I0715405

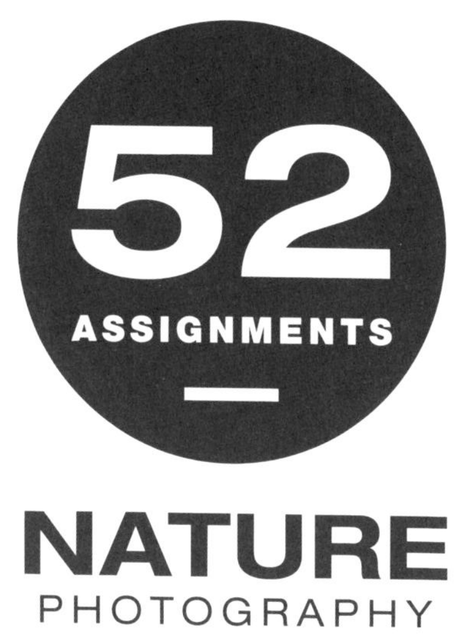

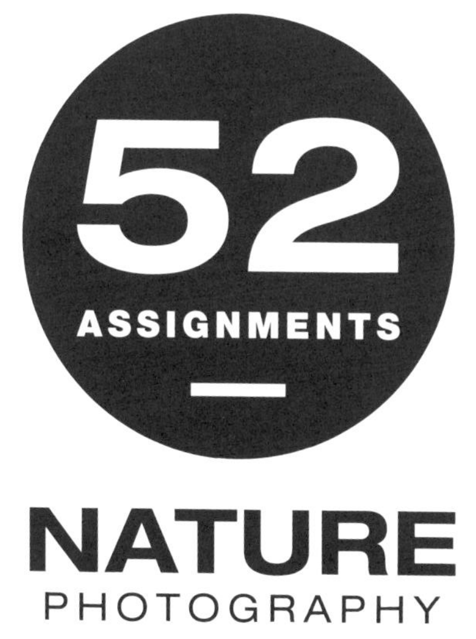

52 ASSIGNMENTS

NATURE
PHOTOGRAPHY

ROSS HODDINOTT & BEN HALL

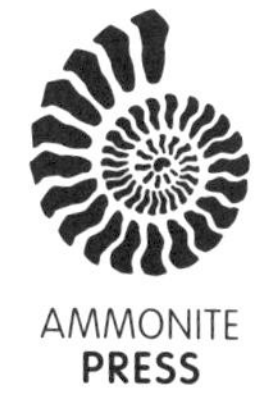

AMMONITE
PRESS

ASSIGNMENTS

Tick off your completed projects

ASSIGNMENT KEY

Each assignment has symbols showing the type of tasks involved.

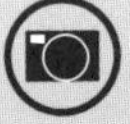 TECHNIQUE

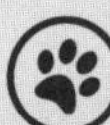 FIELDCRAFT

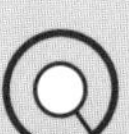 CLOSE-UP

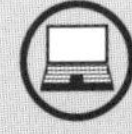 COMPUTER WORK

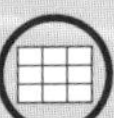 COMPOSITION

 RESEARCH

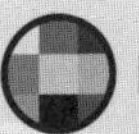 LIGHTING

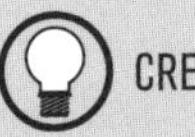 CREATIVITY

ASSIGNMENT JOURNAL

Use the journal spaces throughout the book to keep a record of your experimental assignments and images.

INTRODUCTION

Nature is awe-inspiring, fascinating, and diverse—from the largest mammals to microscopic organisms, from towering trees to peculiar plants, from weird fungi to the huge variety of life underwater. It is hardly surprising that anyone with a camera would want to try to capture all this beauty in a photograph.

But how can you possibly do justice to nature in an image? Can a photographer truly showcase the beauty of the natural world around us? Well, yes, you can, but you will need camera skills, patience, know-how and an innovative approach, as well as a creative eye. And that is exactly how this book can help you. This is a workshop in book form, designed to teach, inspire, and motivate you. Whatever your level of experience—whether you are new to nature photography or a seasoned enthusiast —it remains essential to always be learning, developing, and growing as a photographer.

In this book, we give you a year's worth of weekly assignments. We strongly encourage you to complete them all, but don't worry if it takes you longer than a year, just dip into this book whenever you need inspiration or a fresh concept. Some projects are relatively easy and quick to complete, while others will push you harder and require more time and dedication. You don't need to undertake them in any particular order—just match the assignment to the right subject, situation, and time. By completing them all, you will broaden your horizons, enhance your skills, and become a more able, assured, versatile, and creative nature photographer.

The assignments will give you fresh ideas and arm you with new techniques to help kickstart your creativity and push your nature images to the next level. Nature is a big and diverse subject, and so we cover a broad range of topics within these pages. We will show you how to capture eye-catching images of the animals residing in your own back garden, instruct you on how to build a blind in order to get close to timid subjects, and help you to capture interaction and flight. Whether your subject has six legs, feathers, fur, or flowers, we will guide you in taking better photographs by nurturing your creativity and vision, while providing relevant and essential tips on useful techniques and fieldcraft.

Getting within picture-taking range of wildlife will provide you with many remarkable and memorable encounters. You will learn to appreciate and respect nature even more than you do already. Capturing great nature shots is both rewarding and satisfying, and it also presents you with the opportunity to raise awareness of species and promote the wider cause of wildlife conservation. Never underestimate the power of a picture—do positive things with your photographs and tell your subject's story if you can.

So what are you waiting for? You have your mission brief, now dive in. Use the spaces we've provided to note down your results, observations, hits, and misses, and create your own personalized photo journal to record your journey. Enjoy the challenge, but most of all, enjoy nature…

Ross Hoddinott & Ben Hall

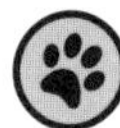

TECHNIQUE

- Take photographs in your garden on dewy mornings or after rainfall. Tiny water droplets will highlight spiders' webs and add scale and sparkle to photographs of mini-beasts.

- Many garden residents are small and inconspicuous, so a macro lens or close-up attachment will be useful.

- Don't overlook everyday, mundane species—even woodlice, small snails, or spiders can look remarkable with a little creativity.

MEET THE LOCALS

For this project, we want you to photograph the wildlife in your own backyard. Gardens—big or small—are home to an abundance of potential photographic subjects which have adapted to urban areas and inhabit our outdoor living space. If you don't have a garden, see if you can adopt a family member's or friend's.

Many gardens contain a number of different habitats—such as hedge, lawn, flower bed, vegetable patch, shrub, rocks, or pond—which will attract a diverse range of wildlife. Start by setting up your own feeding station (see page 14) in order to photograph visiting birds. There are also more secretive creatures living in your backyard. Look under rocks and flowerpots for snails and woodlice, while spiders will decorate a shed and bushes with their webs. Butterflies and bees will visit nectar-rich flowers during summer, and ladybirds and lacewings will hunt aphids and other garden pests in the undergrowth. Your assignment is continued on pages 10–11, where you can discover how to create a wildlife-friendly garden and a wildlife pond, and attract even more photogenic locals to your backyard.

This is an ongoing project. After 12 months, you should have a varied and dynamic portfolio of nature images, taken on your own doorstep.

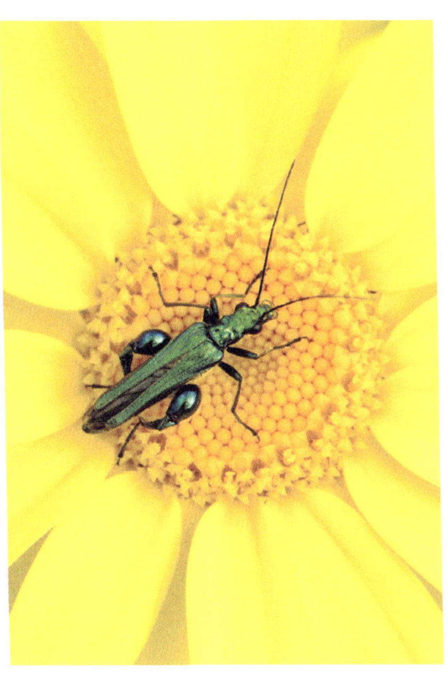

PRO TIPS

• Avoid using pesticides, slug pellets, or any practices that might harm garden residents.

• Woodpiles, compost, and offcuts of wood provide places for little critters to live, feed, and hibernate.

◄ *Look closely, and you will find colorful beetles, bugs, and spiders making themselves at home among your flower beds.*

▼ *Log piles and compost heaps can be home to small mammals and even reptiles. This slowworm was found basking on a rusty sheet of discarded corrugated metal.*

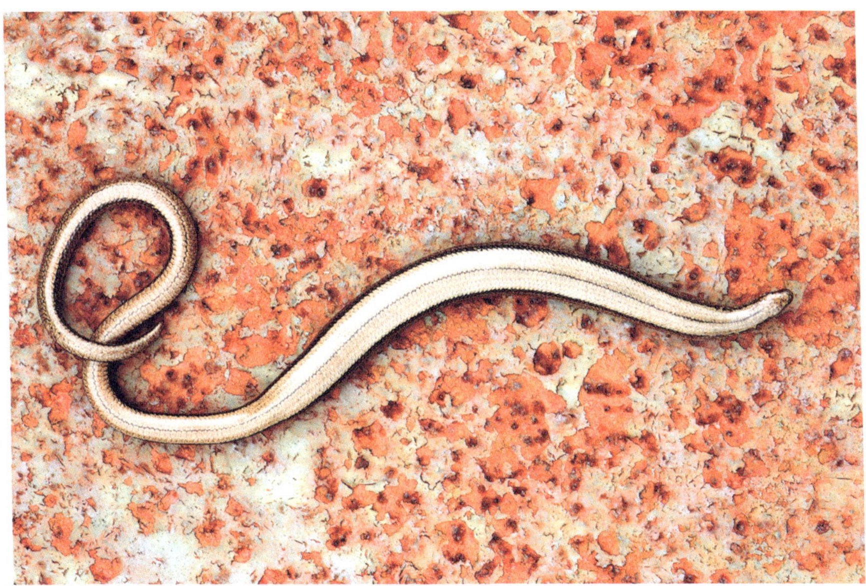

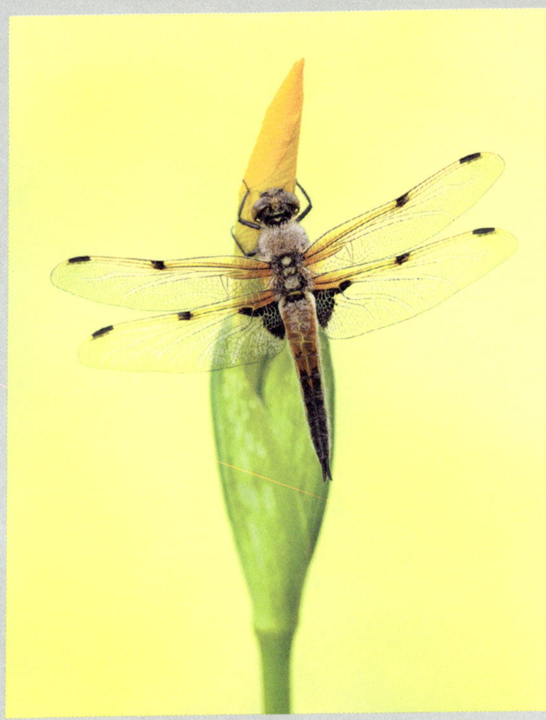

◀ *Dragonflies spend much of their life away from water, so you might spot one hunting in your garden even if you don't have a pond.*

CREATE A WILDLIFE-FRIENDLY GARDEN

You can encourage wildlife into your garden by creating as many different microhabitats as possible:

- Leave a small area of lawn uncut; longer grass is important for insects. Invertebrates are vital to a healthy ecosystem, so, by encouraging them into your garden, you will provide food for birds.

- Fill borders with flowering plants and shrubs that offer nectar for butterflies, bees, and other insects, as well as seeds and berries for birds and small mammals.

- Plant trees and hedges to offer shelter to a variety of creatures and provide places for birds to nest. Climbers on walls will also give insects places to shelter and hibernate.

- If you have space, provide nesting boxes, a hedgehog home, and an insect hotel. There are plenty of online tutorials on how to make your own.

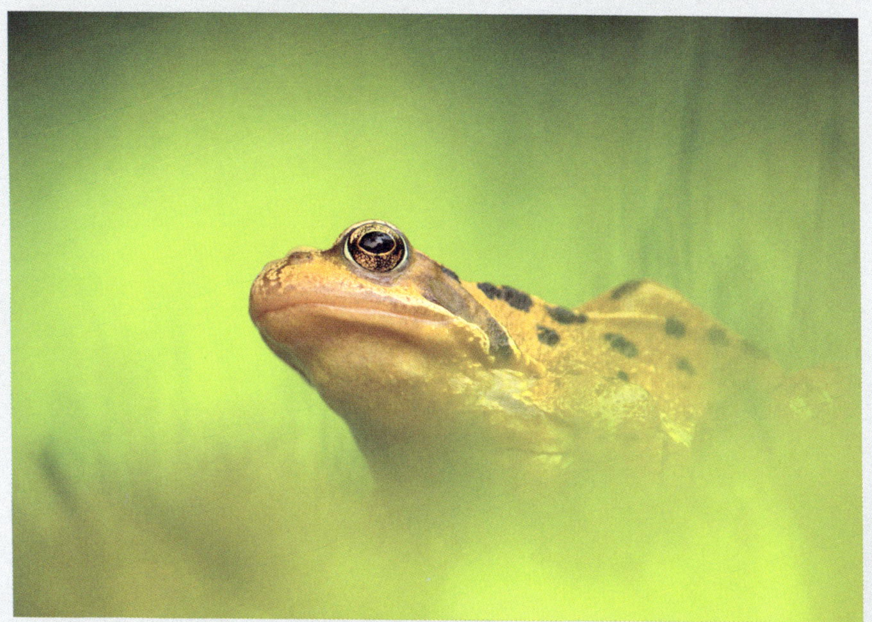

CREATE A WILDLIFE POND

A small pond or water feature will attract wildlife by providing drinking water, somewhere for birds to bathe, and a home for amphibians. Diving beetles, pond skaters, and damselflies will also soon take up residence.

- A pond can be made to fit any space. You can buy preformed ponds made from rigid plastic, which you sink into the ground, or a pond liner. You could even use an old sink or any container that holds water.

- Let your pond fill naturally with rainwater, as tap water contains too many chemicals.

- Ensure there are shallow areas for wildlife to enter and exit safely, and add native aquatic plants (in special pots with mesh sides) and pondweed for cover.

- Keep the water clear at all times by scooping out any leaves or debris with a net.

▲ *Not only will frogs and toads benefit from the creation of a wildlife pond, but you will too, thanks to the photo opportunities they provide.*

WARNING

Remember that even small ponds can be a danger to children—always supervise infants near water.

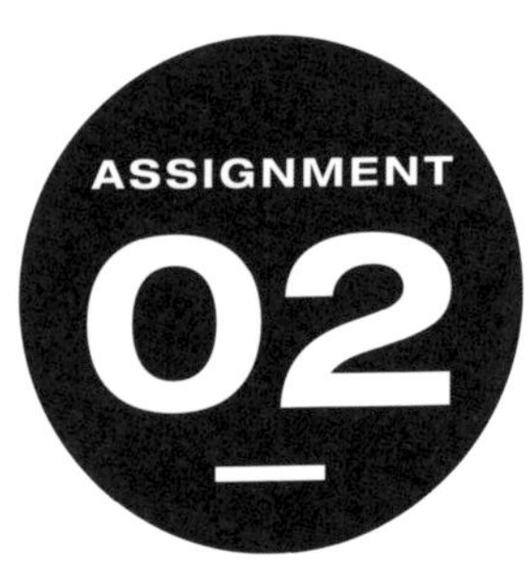

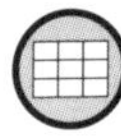

TECHNIQUE

- Experiment with the position of the subject in the frame and the amount of space around it.

- Try using a large aperture to create a shallow depth of field in order to generate a diffused or blurred background, free of clutter, to emphasize the subject.

- It is often best to place more space in front of your subject than behind it—this will direct the viewer's eye to the space into which the subject is looking or moving. It can also be effective to do the opposite and have the subject look away from the space.

NATURAL SPACE

By intentionally recording your subject smaller in the frame and making it less dominant, you can generate "negative space"—the area of the image not occupied by the main subject. This provides breathing space around your subject for it to look, fly, or run into, or shows its habitat.

Creating negative space is simple: use a shorter focal length or move further away from your subject so it is smaller in the frame. This can help provide balance to compositions or enhance symmetry. How much space you include is very much a matter of personal taste. Often, less is more, so don't be afraid to be bold. Minimalist compositions, where the subject is small in the frame, can be compelling and create an impression of solitude, scale, or context.

For this assignment, you simply need to take a photograph of a bird or animal that includes space in the image around it. Shoot a sequence of images of the same subject using varying amounts of negative space, placing the subject at different points in the frame, and select a portfolio of the most effective shots.

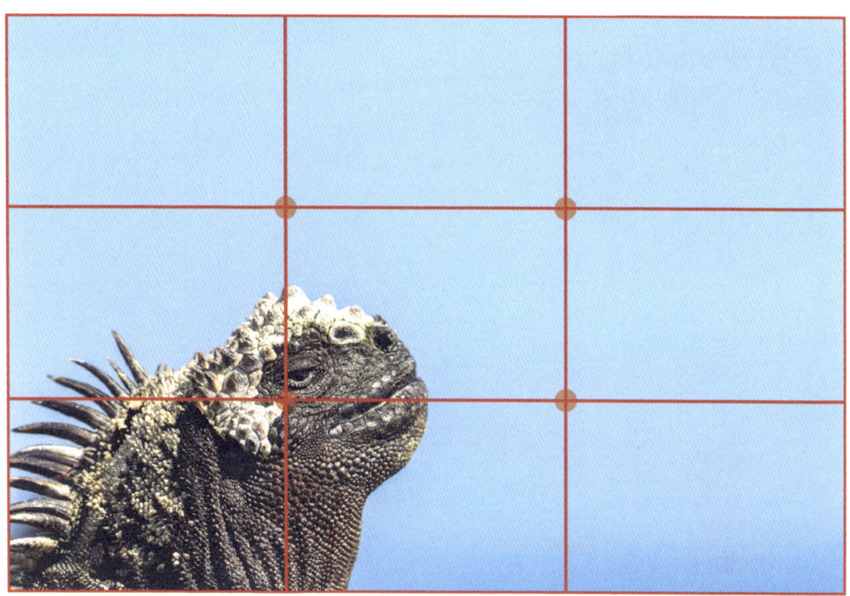

▲ *Think carefully about where to place your subject in the frame. The Rule of Thirds is a helpful guide to applying negative space in an image. Placing your subject on or close to the points at which the lines intersect will often produce the most striking compositions.*

▼ *By recording your subject smaller in the frame, you can convey more about the subject and where it lives.*

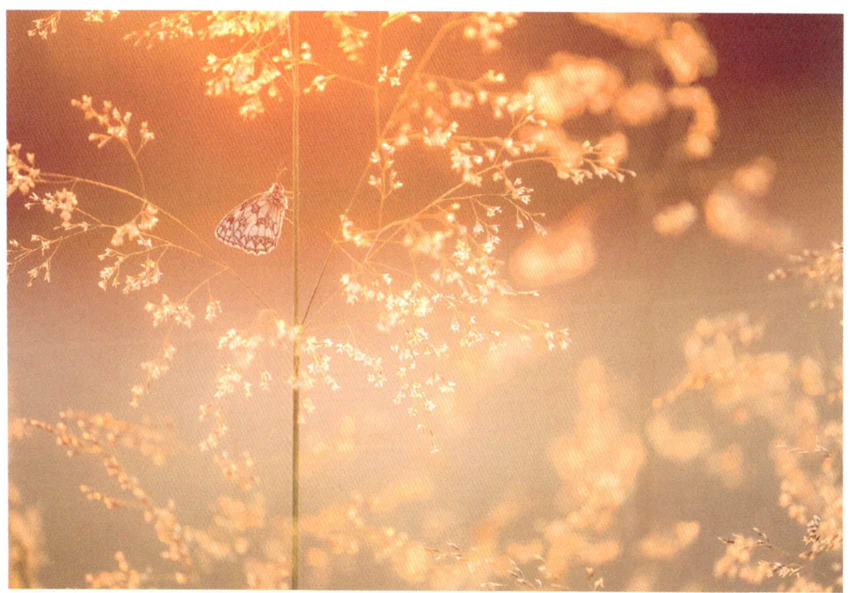

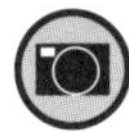

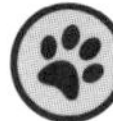

TECHNIQUE

- Some small birds, such as tits and finches, move incredibly quickly. Keep your shutter speed to a minimum of 1/800 sec. to achieve critical sharpness.

- If you struggle to find a suitable natural background, try making a false background out of material in a subdued color. This can be used to disguise objects such as fences or sheds for more natural-looking images.

FIELD NOTES

- Consider the position of the sun as it rises and sets. Place your feeders so you can shoot front-lit and backlit images at different times of the day.

- Different types of food can be used to attract a variety of bird species. Nuts, sesame seeds, fat balls, and mealworms are all great options.

FEEDING TIME

A good feeding station can turn your back garden into a haven for wild birds, giving you endless opportunities for nature photography all year round. It doesn't need to be complex—keep things simple and it will be easier to maintain. Set up a single pole and attach one or two feeders to it. For natural-looking images, avoid including the feeders in the frame at all costs. Instead, buy a set of spring clamps and use them to attach natural perches to the pole. Birds will often land momentarily on these perches before hopping down onto the feeders, giving you the chance to capture simple, yet striking, portrait images. When positioning your feeders, pay close attention to the background. Ideally, it should be distant enough to be rendered completely out of focus when using a wide aperture, and consist of foliage that would match the birds' natural habitat. Once you are happy with taking portrait images, why not challenge yourself to capture some action shots of specific behavior, such as squabbling.

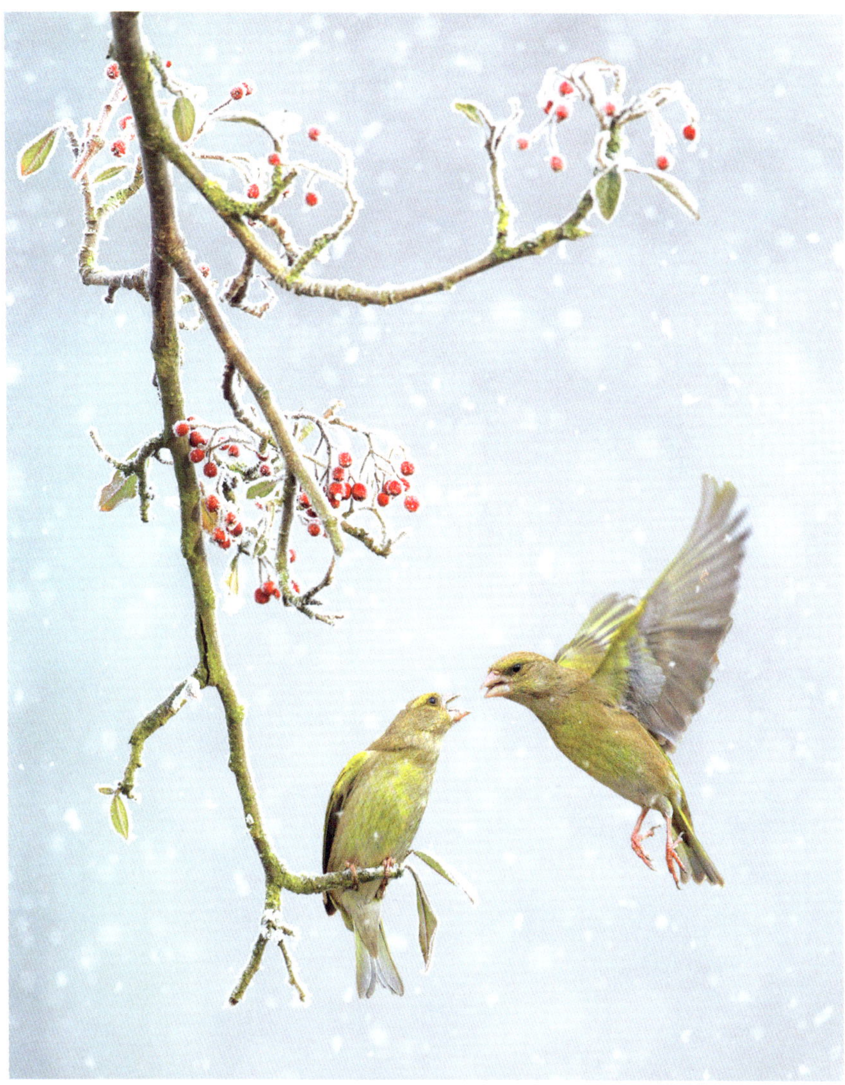

PRO TIPS

- Use the high-speed drive mode on your camera to enable you to fire a burst of frames, giving you a better chance of capturing the right moment.

- To freeze small birds in flight you will need to increase your shutter speed even further, to at least 1/2000 sec.

▲ *Winter weather will often bring a greater number of birds, increasing your chances of capturing behavior like this.*

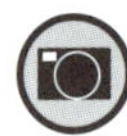

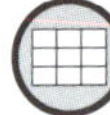

TECHNIQUE

- When shooting a moving subject using a slow shutter speed, panning technique is critical. Hone your skills with faster shutter speeds before attempting motion blur.

- A tripod with a gimbal head can be a useful tool for panning. It eliminates the weight of the lens but allows smooth movement.

- A large flock of geese taking flight or a starling murmuration are both subjects that would suit images depicting motion.

- One added benefit of selecting a slow shutter speed is that it will allow you to use a lower ISO setting than usual, helping you to achieve the cleanest image possible.

▼ *A shutter speed of 1/5 sec. was used to capture the motion in the gull's wings. Often, images taken with a slow shutter speed take on a painterly quality (see page 116).*

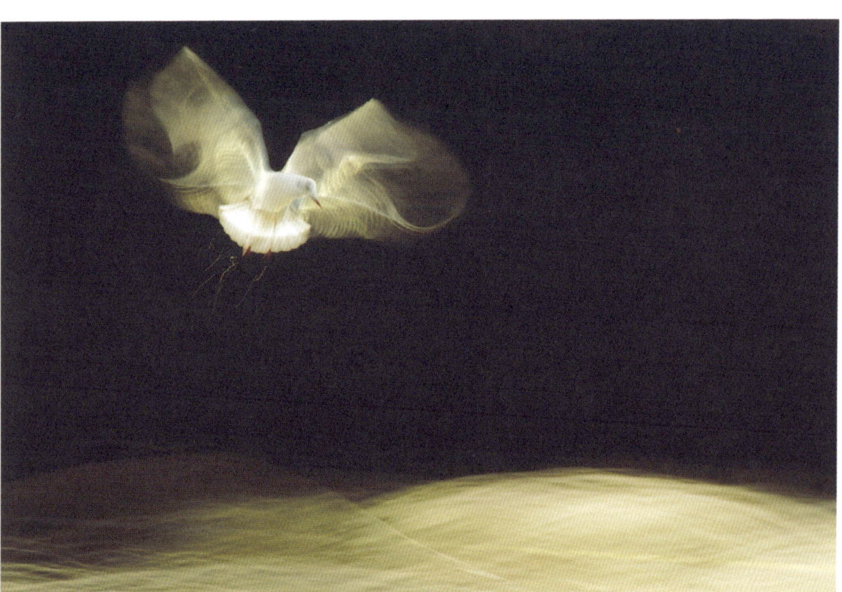

SLOW THE PACE

For this assignment, we want you to capture a series of images of a creature in motion. You will need to experiment a great deal, and you must be prepared for a low success rate. But get it right and the resulting images can be beautifully artistic, revealing an aspect of the subject that is impossible to see with the human eye. So, get creative, forget rules and boundaries, and let your imagination take over.

The approach we're asking you to try here is to create blur intentionally by using a relatively slow shutter speed. Select shutter priority mode and set the shutter speed to between 1/15 and 1/60 sec. Depending on the speed and distance of your subject, you may need to increase or decrease the shutter speed. There are no set rules—experiment until you find a setting that works. The slower the shutter speed, the more abstract your images will appear. Even though your subject may not be recognizable, the resulting images can look beautiful.

▼ *This red hartebeest and its young were captured using a shutter speed of 1/15 sec.— fast enough to freeze the subject, but slow enough to create a sense of speed due to the motion-blur effect in the background.*

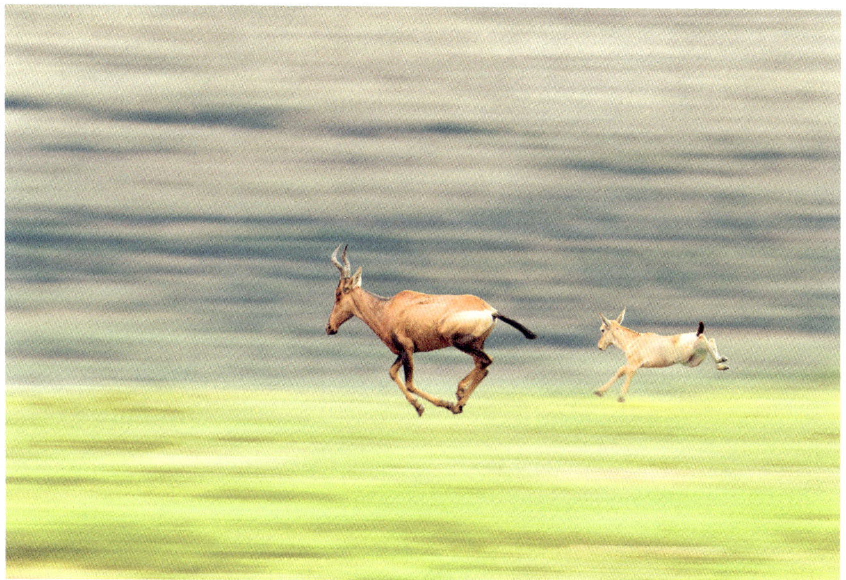

TECHNIQUE

- Many digital SLRs allow you to expand the focus area by activating more than one focus point, which increases your margin for error when tracking a moving subject.

- If shooting against the sky, the camera will be fooled into underexposing. Add between one and three stops of positive exposure compensation to prevent the bird becoming a silhouette.

FIELD NOTES

- If flight photography is new to you, practice on large birds—such as swans, geese, and herons—which offer a larger target, and tend to fly slowly and predictably compared to smaller birds.

FLIGHTS OF FANCY

Your brief for this assignment is to photograph a bird in flight. This might sound simple enough, but is in fact one of the most challenging briefs in nature photography. There are plenty of technical aspects to worry about but don't let this hamper your creativity. Learn the technicalities until they are second nature. You will then be free to concentrate on other important factors such as lighting and choice of background.

One vital ingredient is panning technique. Stand with your feet shoulder-width apart and tuck in the elbow of whichever hand is holding the lens to create a stable support. As you follow your subject, swivel the upper half of your body in one fluid movement, matching the speed of the bird. Activate the predictive focus mode to enable your camera to track the subject. Use the high-speed drive mode to fire a burst of images as you pan, to give you a sequence of pictures to choose from.

Shooting in strong light is ideal as it will allow a fast shutter speed, but avoid the harsh light that occurs around midday. Cloudy or stormy conditions can also work well—a bird lit by the sun against a dark sky can look truly spectacular.

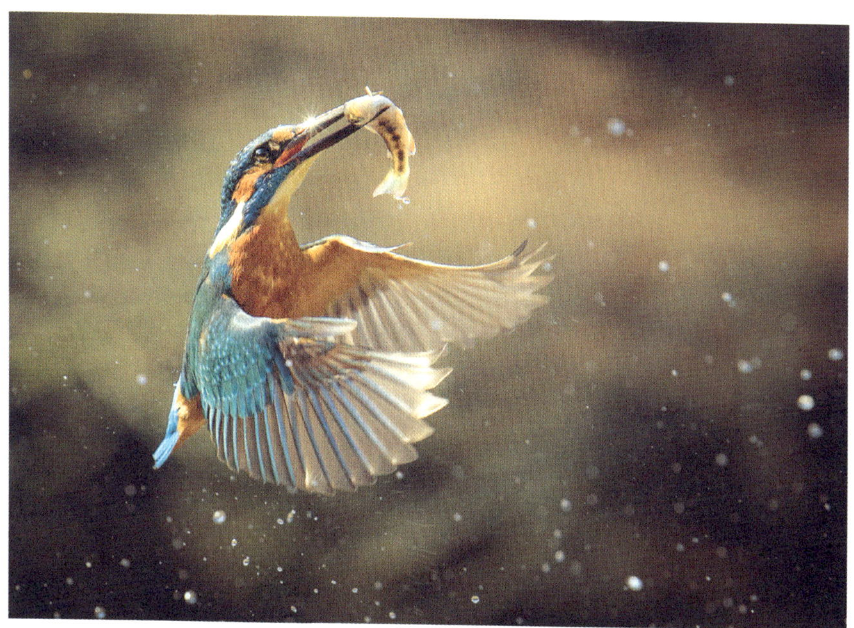

▲ Aim for a shutter speed of at least 1/1000 sec. to freeze medium- to large-sized birds in flight. Smaller birds fly incredibly quickly so you may need a higher shutter speed than 1/2000 sec.

▼ Shooting when the sun is low in the sky will light the underside of the bird. This will reveal plenty of feather detail, adding definition and interest to your subject.

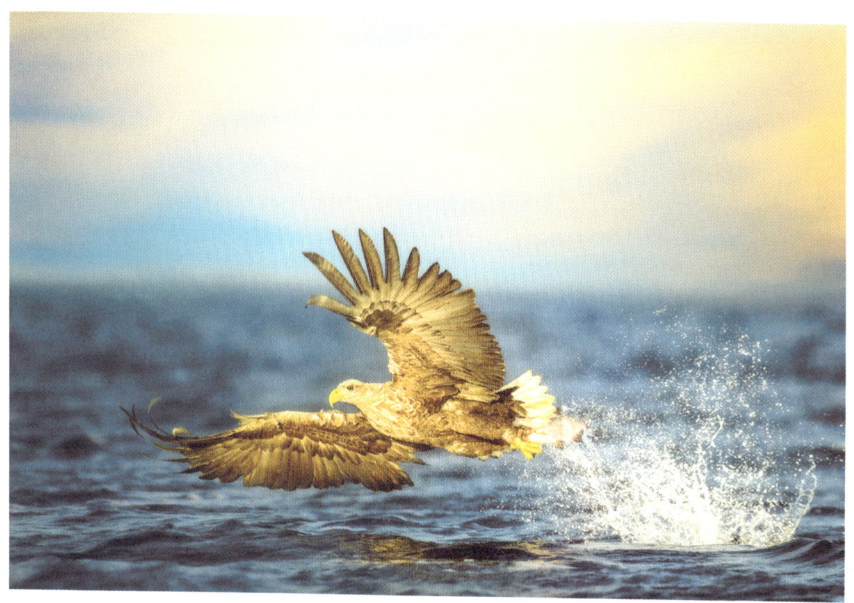

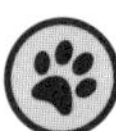
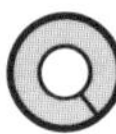

TECHNIQUE

- Close-up filters can be used with any lens, but a 70–200mm telephoto zoom lens is often a good choice and will help create a practical working distance.

- Check the filter thread size of your lens and buy a close-up filter that matches.

- At higher magnifications, depth of field is shallow, so always focus precisely.

FIELD NOTES

- Extension tubes are a low-cost alternative—they fit between camera and lens to reduce the lens's minimum focusing distance. Reversing rings are another good option.

UNSEEN NATURE

To capture frame-filling shots of miniature subjects, you need a close-focusing lens, capable of high magnification. The obvious choice is a dedicated macro lens—a specialist lens optimized for close-focusing. However, for this assignment we want you to shoot several images using a close-up filter, which converts existing lenses into close-focusing ones.

Normal lenses have a minimum focusing distance in the region of 3–10ft (1–3m), making them unsuitable for close-up photography. A close-up filter will convert your standard optics into powerful close-focusing devices, allowing you to photograph smaller subjects. Available in a variety of strengths and lens diameters, they work like a magnifying glass, screwing onto the front of a standard lens and reducing its minimum focusing distance to increase magnification. Close-up filters are compact, lightweight, and don't reduce the light entering the camera, and they can be attached or detached in an instant. They can't quite match the optical quality of a macro lens, but they can provide good results, particularly at mid-range apertures, such as f/8. Your assignment is continued on pages 22–3 with a guide to focusing for close-up images.

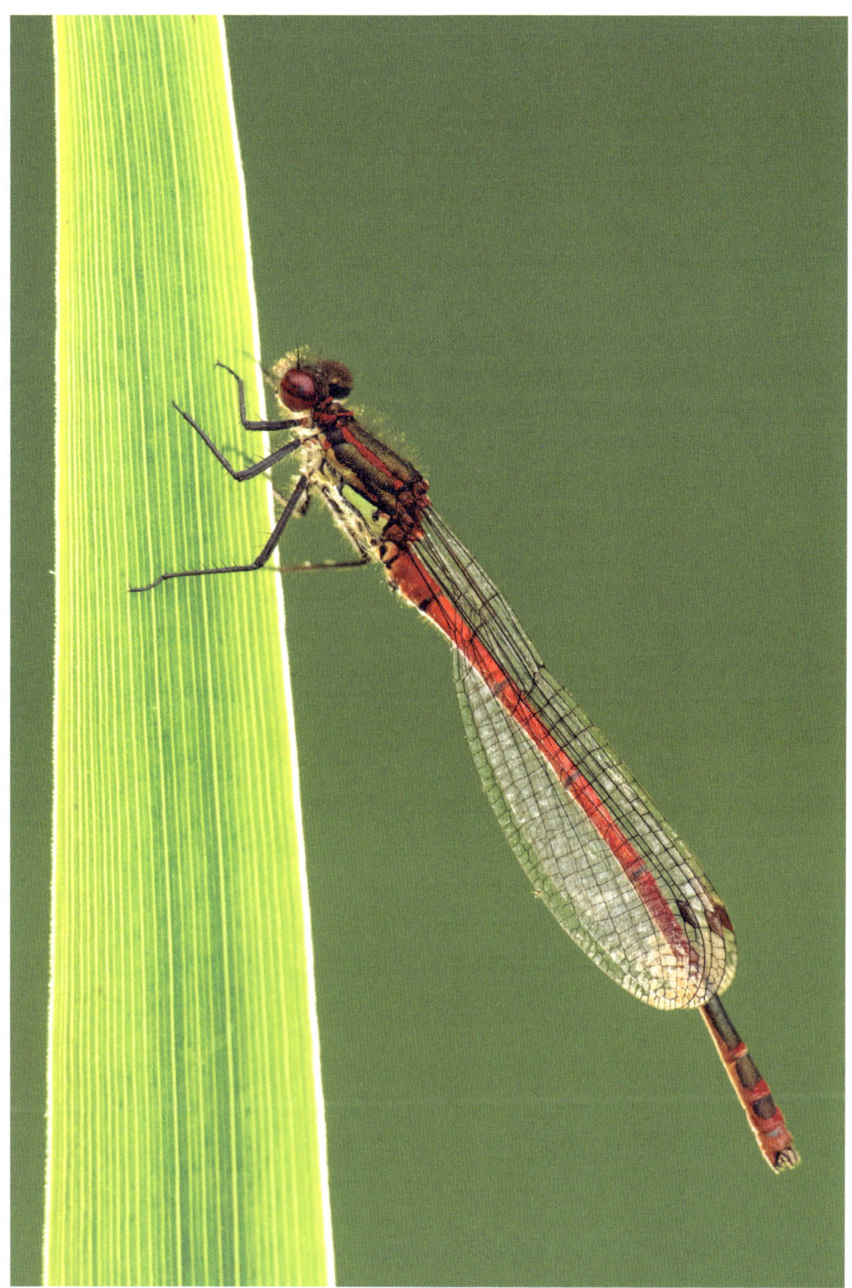

▲ *Most close-up filters are marked with their diopter value to indicate their strength, for example, +1, +2, +3, or +4, with larger numbers representing greater effective magnification.*

IMPROVE YOUR FOCUS

The secret to great close-ups is acquiring focus. Follow this guide
and create your own series of shots to complete the assignment.

• Be prepared to get quite close to subjects, typically within 12in
(30cm). Always approach with care, avoiding sudden, jerky
movements so as not to disturb timid subjects, such as flighty insects.

• Switch to manual focusing. Autofocus can struggle to lock on to
nearby objects, particularly in low light.

• Your focusing will need to be pin-point accurate, with depth of field
being shallow at high magnifications. Whenever possible, use a
tripod and activate Live View. Magnify your intended point of focus,
such as the subject's eye, for precise focusing.

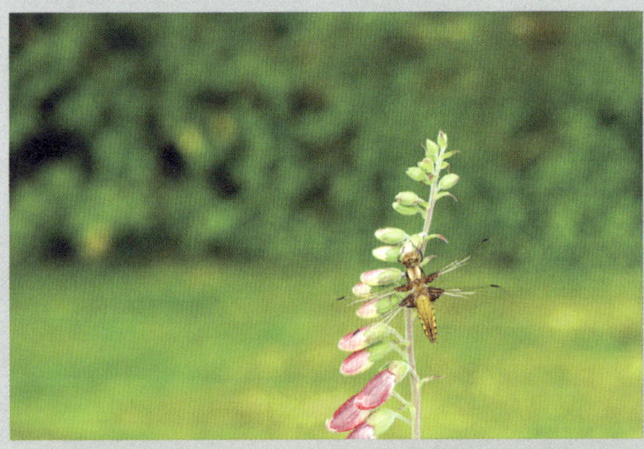

◄ *This image of a
broad-bodied chaser
dragonfly was shot with
a 70–200mm lens, close
to the lens's minimum
focusing distance (the lens's
maximum magnification)
without a close-up filter.*

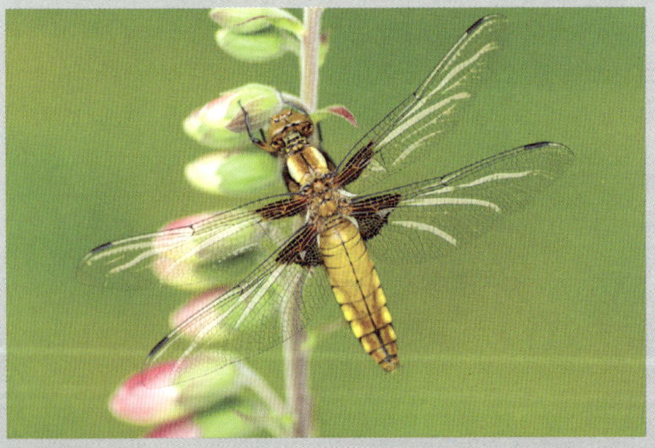

◄ *With a NiSi NC close-up
filter attached, the lens is
able to focus closer and
frame-filling results become
more achievable.*

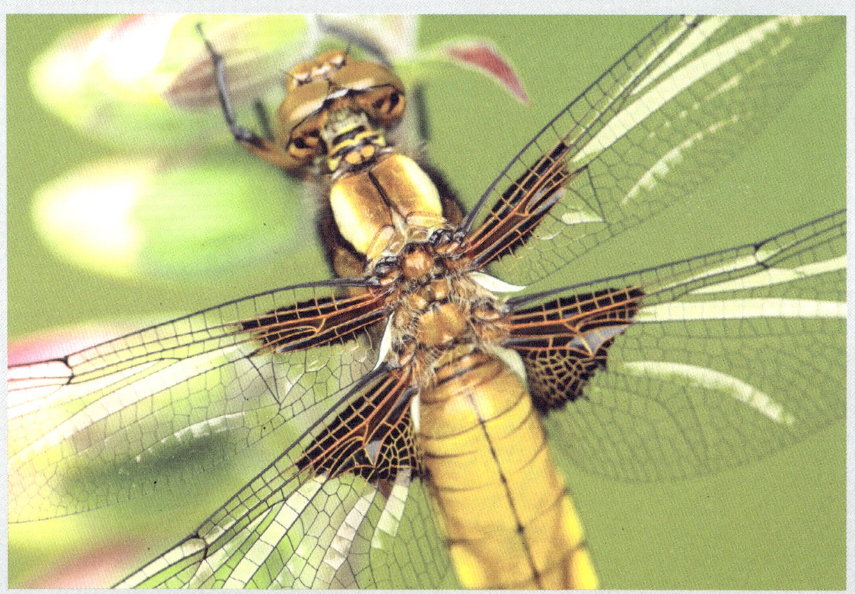

▲ By physically moving the camera about 6in (15cm) closer to the subject, it is possible to achieve an even higher level of magnification.

▼ By moving closer again, with the lens at 200mm and set to its minimum focusing distance, it is possible to achieve the maximum level of magnification for this setup.

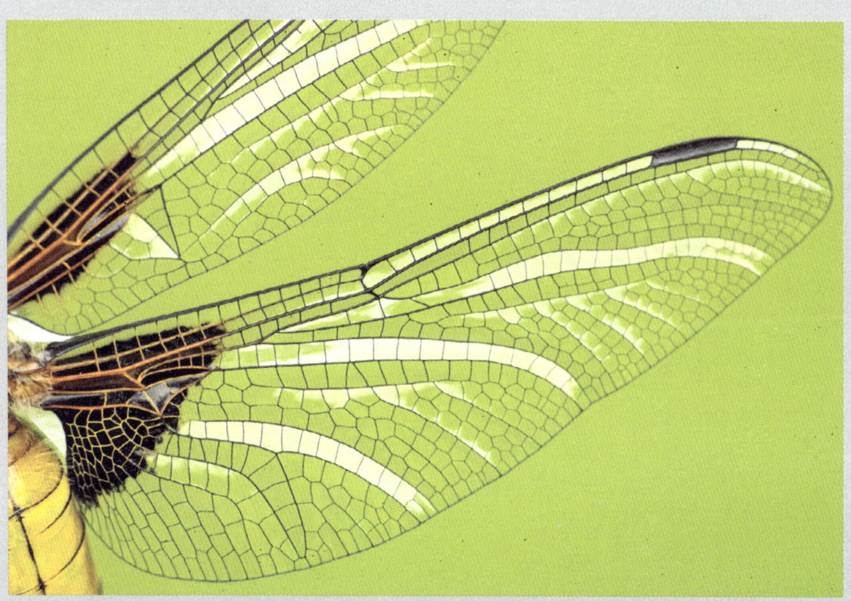

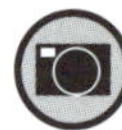

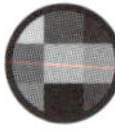

TECHNIQUE

- Keep an eye on the histogram. Backlighting can sometimes fool the camera into underexposing, so use a small amount of positive exposure compensation to ensure maximum detail is held in the shadows.

- If shooting against a dark background, try to underexpose the image so that just the rim-light is visible and the rest of the image is rendered completely black. About 2–3 stops of negative exposure compensation should do it.

- Avoid lens flare by not shooting directly towards the sun and using a lens hood.

▼ *Purposely underexposing a subject against a dark background can produce simple but stunning results.*

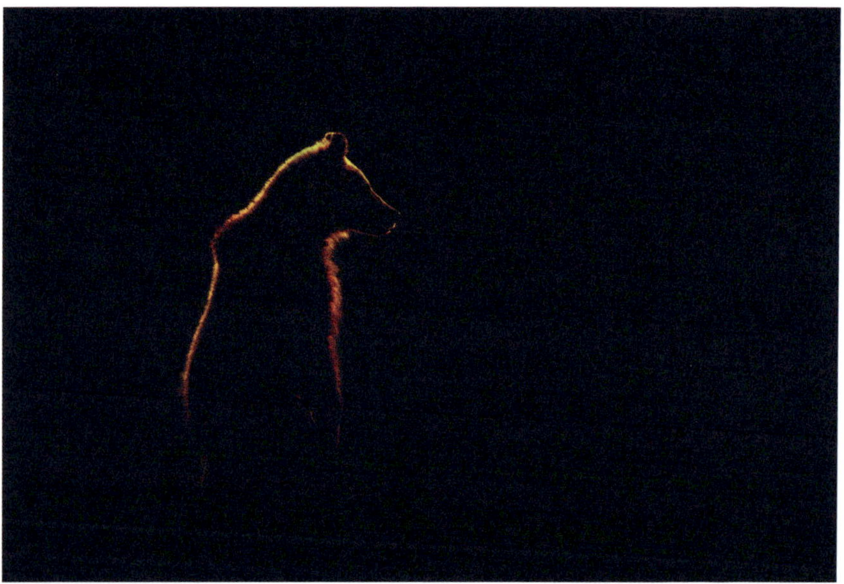

BACKLIT BEASTS

Photographing a subject with backlighting will highlight its shape and form, adding atmosphere and evoking emotion. This is most effective when the sun is close to the horizon, during the first and last minutes of sunlight—contrast levels are reduced and the light temperature is warmer, eliminating strong shadows and harsh highlights.

Your brief here is to visit an open environment, such as your local park, just after first light or an hour or two before sunset, and search for interesting subjects that are lit by the sun. Position yourself so that the sun is in front of you but slightly off to one side. This way, you will create the most desirable by-product of backlighting, which is called rim-lighting. This is where the sun lights up the outline of the subject, highlighting its shape and form. With a suitable subject and the right light, the results can be truly magical, but be careful to avoid flare.

Mammals with fur coats work well when the hairs are rim-lit by the sun, and the almost translucent feathers of backlit birds can also look spectacular. There is no shortage of subjects to experiment with, so get out there and chase the light. Try to find a subject that appeals to you, and create a composition with your own personal approach. Complete your assignment by printing a pair of your best backlit beasts.

▼ Backlighting your subject on a cold morning will often reveal their breath. Where possible, shoot against a dark background to ensure the breath is clearly visible in the image.

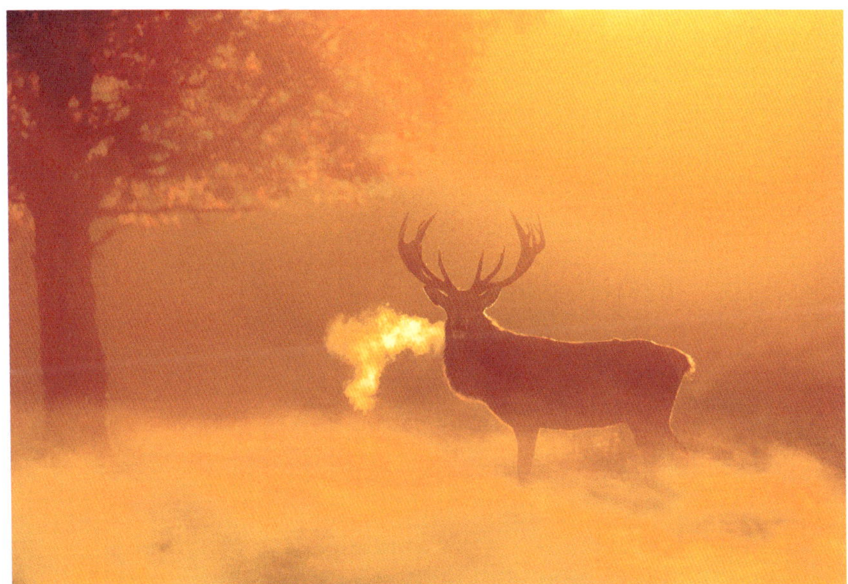

"

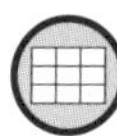

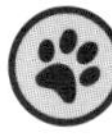

TECHNIQUE

- At a low angle it may be easier to use your camera's articulated LCD screen to compose your image using Live View.

- Resting your lens on a beanbag offers all the support you need and makes setting up quick and easy.

- Be careful not to obscure too much of your subject. Avoid vegetation that distracts from or covers key parts, such as the eyes.

WORM'S-EYE VIEW

For this assignment, be prepared to get down and dirty. We want you to lie down on the ground and take a photograph of nature at a low level. Lying down reduces disturbance and allows you to capture more intimate and striking images of nature. It is also an excellent way to create a natural eye-to-eye perspective.

A worm's-eye view emphasizes your subject, and helps you to obscure clutter and distraction by reducing the foreground and background to a hazy blur. By shooting with your lens at ground level, you will obscure almost all recognizable detail either side of the lens's plane of focus. This is because, when you lie down, you place extra distance between the subject and its background, so it becomes more out of focus. For example, a messy or distracting surface—such as grass, water, fallen leaves, snow, or sand—will be rendered so out of focus that it simply records as a wash of color, producing a far more aesthetically pleasing result than from shooting higher up.

This technique is best applied with a telephoto lens with a focal length of more than 300mm, together with a large aperture. The narrow zone of focus created by this combination will help your subject really pop out of the picture. Your focusing will need to be pin-point accurate—always focus on an animal's eye.

So now set out to capture a series of four ground-level images and share them on your website or social media feed (see page 122).

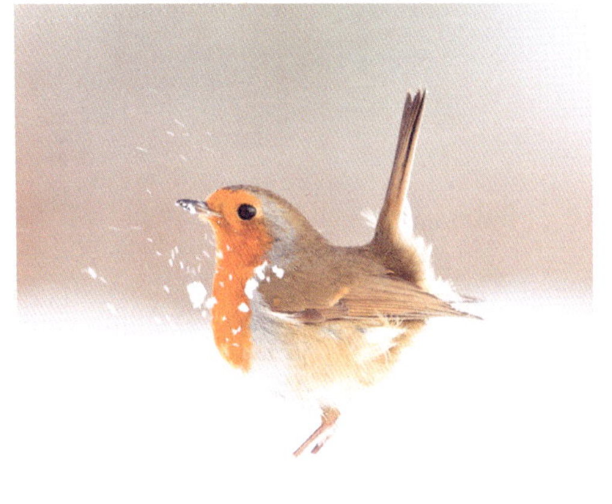

▲ *A low viewpoint and long lens will throw everything but your subject out of focus.*

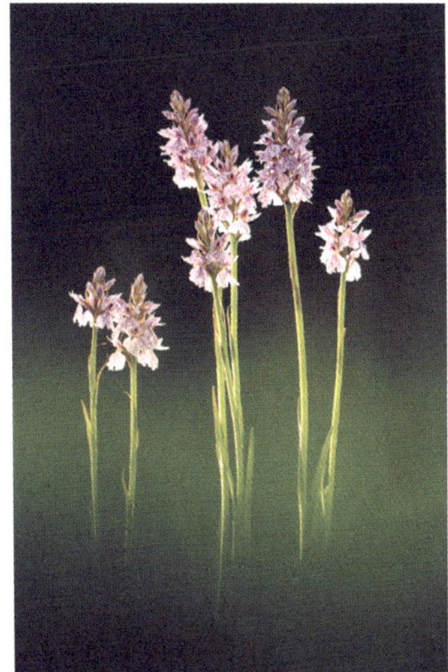

▲ *Low-level photography can be uncomfortable for the photographer, but the results can look bold and extremely intimate.*

ASSIGNMENT JOURNAL

FIELD NOTES

- Depending on the terrain, time of year, and weather, shooting from ground level can be dirty work. Wear suitable clothing, or, if the opportunity allows, use a groundsheet of some sort.

- Ground-level photography can suit all wildlife, but particularly birds, mammals, reptiles, wild flowers, and fungi.

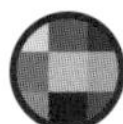
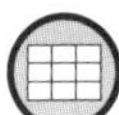

TECHNIQUE

- Knowing which subject will suit the high-key technique is important. Look for pale animals against pale surroundings.

- When exposing to the right, ensure that your highlights do not bleed over the right-hand edge of the histogram, meaning a loss of detail.

PRO TIPS

- High-key images can look slightly washed out on the camera's LCD screen, but adding some blacks at the post-processing stage will deepen the contrast and add punch.

SEE THE LIGHT

Photographs that are made up of mainly pale tones and colors are known as "high-key" images. They have an esthetic quality to them that exemplifies simplicity. For this project, we are asking you to take an almost monochromatic approach to create some striking high-key photographs.

Exposing for high-key images is fairly straightforward. You will need to employ a technique known as "exposing to the right." This means that you may need to add enough positive exposure compensation so the histogram just nudges the right-hand edge of the graph. This ensures that maximum detail is held in both the shadows and the highlights, but at the whitest end of the visual spectrum.

The trick for successful high-key images is learning to visualize the final image and knowing when to employ the technique. Winter scenes provide an ideal opportunity, when snow covers the ground, for instance. Find a white subject, such as a mountain hare, and photograph it against the white of the snow, or perhaps a white bird against a pale, featureless sky—both create a sense of intrigue and mystery. Now find your own pale subjects against pale backgrounds, photograph a set of high-key images, and print the two most effective ones.

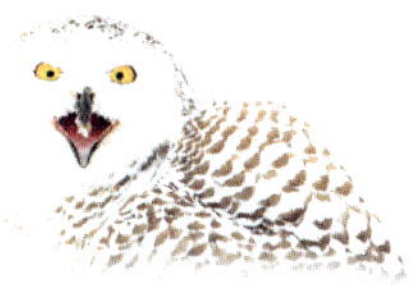

▲ *The whites appear almost pure white in this image, but the histogram shows that the details are still there. The blacks on the plumage of the bird add contrast and impact.*

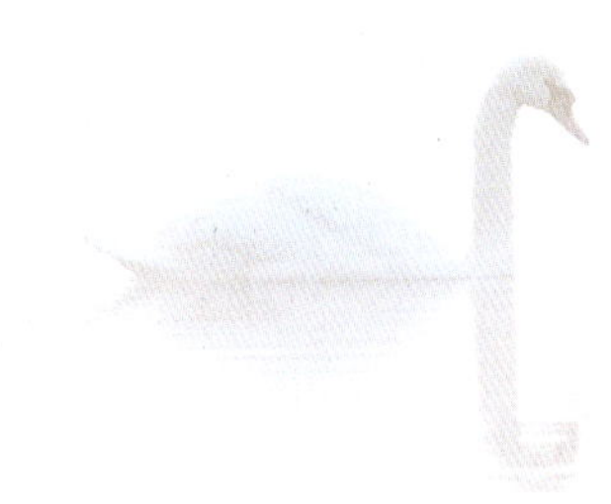

▲ *The lack of detail in this image encourages the viewer to focus on the elegant form of the swan.*

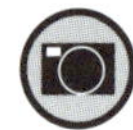
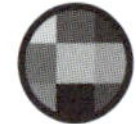
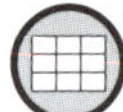

TECHNIQUE

- Pick a dark subject and look for an area of shadow you can aim your camera toward. This will act as the background and help create dramatic results.

- The histogram is invaluable when creating low-key images. Check it regularly to ensure that your exposure is as near as it can be to the left-hand side of the graph.

- Make sure the histogram doesn't bleed over the left-hand edge of the graph as well, to ensure that shadow detail is still present, even if it is not immediately visible.

- Increasing the whites at the post-processing stage is an essential part of getting the most out of your low-key images. This will increase your image's contrast and punch.

▼ *This image of a jaguar stalking its prey was taken in Brazil, in bright sunlight. By dialing in -3 stops of exposure compensation, I eliminated the distracting foliage and emphasized the dappled sunlight on the jaguar, capturing its intensity and power.*

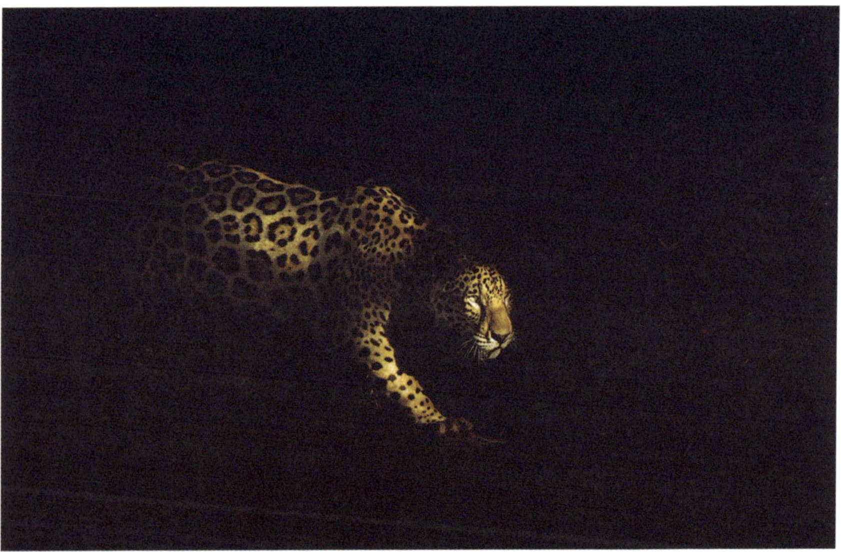

INTO THE DARKNESS

"Low-key" images consist of mostly dark tones and colors and they create a sense of drama, atmosphere, and mystery. So, your brief here is to find a dark subject against dark surroundings, and experiment with exposure. Sometimes less obvious subjects can work well, too—search for birds or animals that are lit by the sun and try to position yourself so that you are shooting towards an area of shadow.

You may need to add negative exposure compensation to prevent the camera from overexposing the image. Check the histogram and start with -1 stop, lowering this until the histogram nudges the left-hand side. This ensures that the original, uncompressed RAW file from your camera will always closely resemble the post-processed image—important if you are entering your images into competitions for which RAW files are requested for authentication purposes (see page 124).

To complete the assignment, find an animal or bird in a dark setting and experiment with your exposure settings to create your own dramatic portrait of the subject. Once you have a set of images you're happy with, print off the best two.

▼ This goldeneye duck was swimming under some overhanging branches which created deep shadows on the water. After dialing in some negative exposure compensation, the water appears almost black.

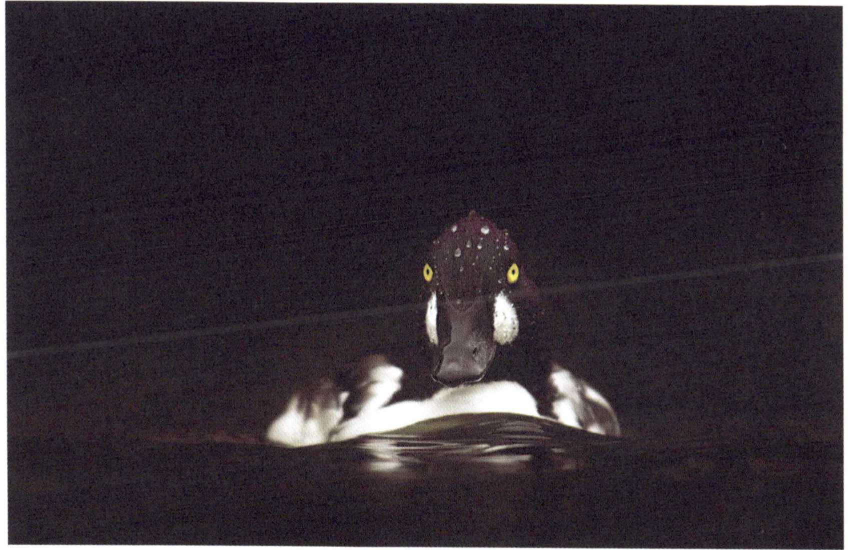

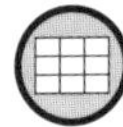

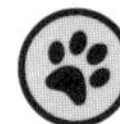

TECHNIQUE

- Environmental images depend greatly on the suitability of the surroundings. Deer in forests or parks, seabird colonies on cliffs, or mountain-dwelling animals, for instance, are all suitable subjects.

- A telephoto zoom lens, such as a 70–200mm or 100–400mm, will give you much-needed flexibility for framing.

- Wideangle lenses will allow you to include the environment in your images with your subject, provided you can approach closely enough.

- If using wideangle lenses, you will need to approach your subject very carefully. Make no sudden movements and keep your profile low.

- A lower shooting angle nearly always results in a more effective image.

WILDLIFE LANDSCAPE

A portrait that fills the frame may have instant impact, but a photograph that shows a creature in the landscape tells a story. For this assignment, think carefully about your subject and come up with interesting ways of featuring it within its environment. If you are accustomed to automatically getting as close as possible, you will need to rethink your whole approach. Try to start thinking like a landscape photographer, but use the bird or animal as the point of interest.

Composition is crucial. Look for features within the landscape that can be used to frame the subject, or leading lines that draw the viewer's eye to it. You are trying to capture the scene in front of you, but with the animal as the defining element within it. When concentrating on the environment, it is likely that the creature will appear small in the frame, but it is important that it does not become lost in the picture. Try to place the subject over an area of diffuse color, or against a featureless part of the landscape. Think carefully about what to include and what to eliminate, and study every inch of the frame. Moving just a few meters in either direction can make a dramatic difference to the background and its effectiveness.

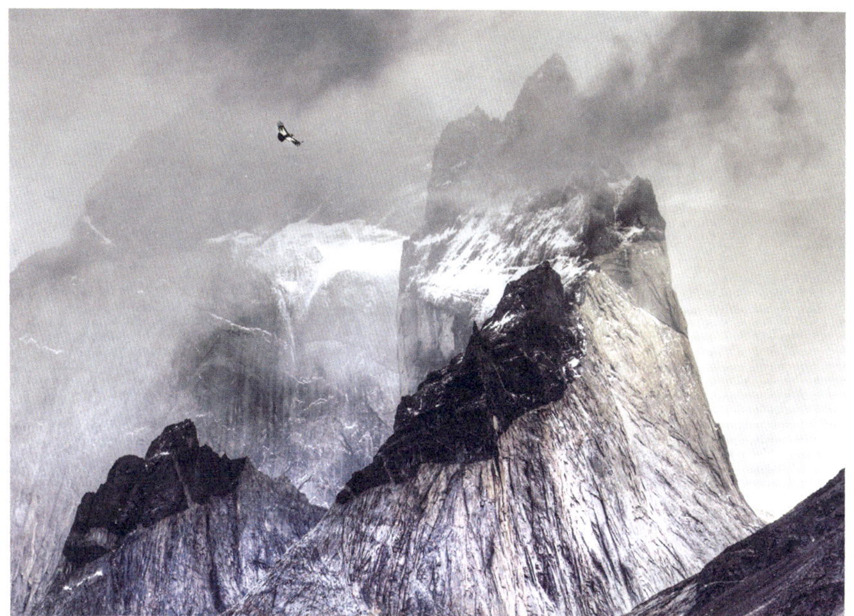

▲ Although the bird appears small in the frame, it is instantly visible. The mountain ridge acts as a leading line, snaking across the frame to the condor.

▼ The tree acts as a natural frame, and the deer is placed against a featureless part of the background.

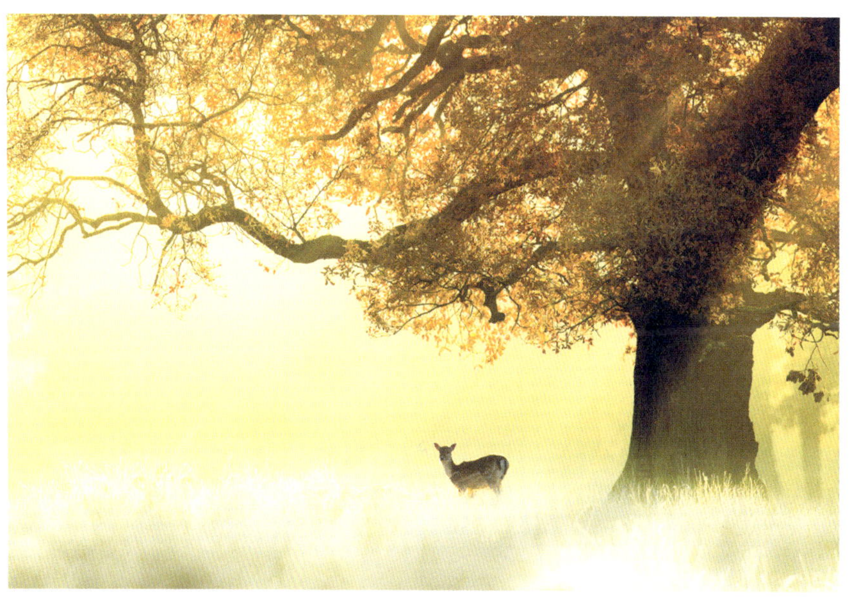

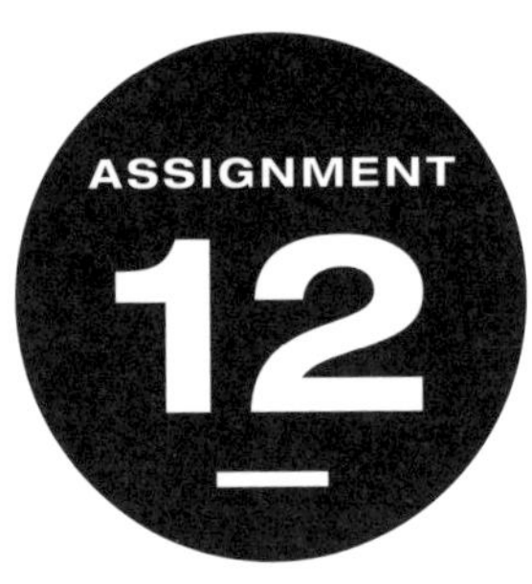

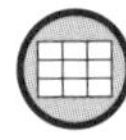
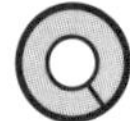

TECHNIQUE

- Study subjects closely and look for contrast, color, unusual detail, and symmetry. It is the subject's form that is important, not its surroundings.

- Look for geometric shapes, lines, and repeating patterns—these are the most photogenic forms to photograph.

- Crop in tightly to your subject and fill the frame. Disguising scale and context helps to highlight color, shape, and form.

NATURE'S ABSTRACTS

This assignment is all about focusing on the small details and using your creative eye to find interesting patterns, repetition, shapes, forms, and natural textures. Your brief is to shoot three contrasting close-ups. Don't worry about realism. Subjects become increasingly abstracted the more you crop into them, and that is the idea—to produce your own, unique, creative close-ups. You shouldn't need to go far to find exquisite miniature detail, but you will probably need to employ a high level of magnification to highlight color and texture. So, think about using a macro lens or close-up attachment (see page 20).

Exclude anything from the frame that is a distraction. Lines are often a powerful compositional tool, particularly when placed diagonally. Light will help shape your subject and create depth; but often diffused, even light will record color and detail most faithfully. Developing an eye for shooting nature's abstracts can take time, but completing this assignment will accelerate the process.

ASSIGNMENT JOURNAL

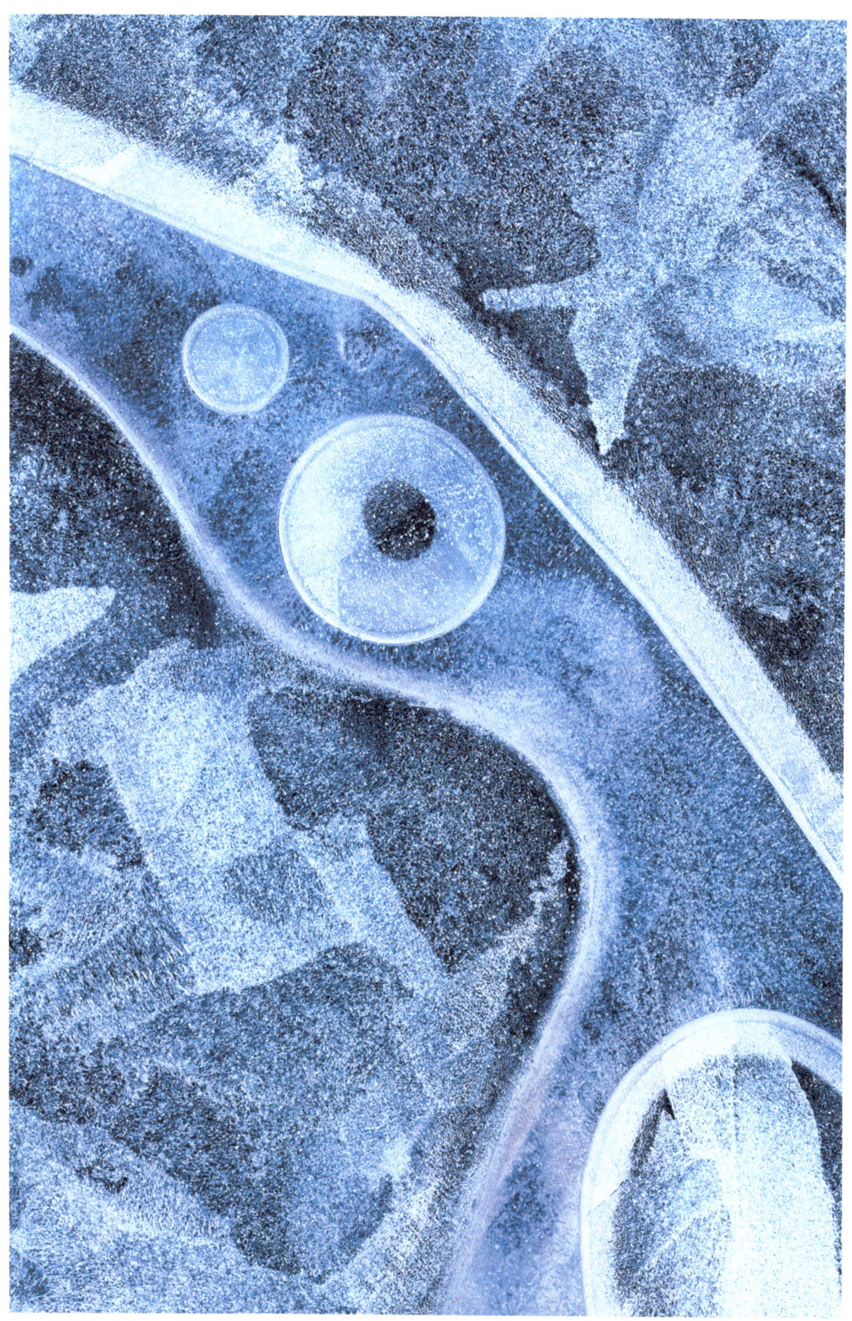

▲ *When shooting abstracts, technique is arguably less important than the ability to "see" the beauty in nature's rich and varied forms.*

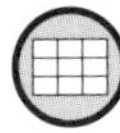

TECHNIQUE

- First, study and understand the basic rules of composition, so you can then break them for this assignment.

- Learn to frame your subjects intuitively, rather than being constrained by preconceived ideas. Composition is a highly subjective thing, but creative experimentation is an important part of growing as a photographer.

PRO TIP

- Whether you adhere to rules or break them, the best advice is to keep it simple. Frames that are cluttered, fussy, and chaotic rarely succeed.

BREAK THE RULES

If you follow compositional guidelines slavishly, you risk your images becoming contrived, predictable, and unimaginative. Many of the best, standout nature photographs are fresh, original, and unconventional. Sometimes ignoring the rulebook altogether is the best approach, but don't do so for the sake of it. Continue to adhere to the rules when it is appropriate for the subject, but ignore them whenever the opportunity allows. The key to good composition is often balance. Applying the Rule of Thirds (see page 12) will often create well-balanced, harmonious compositions, but sometimes placing your subject in the center of the frame creates more impact. In images that include the horizon, try placing it closer to the bottom of the frame rather than on a third. This can create a heightened sense of isolation and scale.

We recommend you work with just one species for this project. Take a series of photographs depicting it both large and small within the image space, positioned in different parts of the frame, and with bold use of negative space. Try combining different approaches to create daring and unconventional compositions. Completing this assignment will help you learn so much about what does and doesn't work.

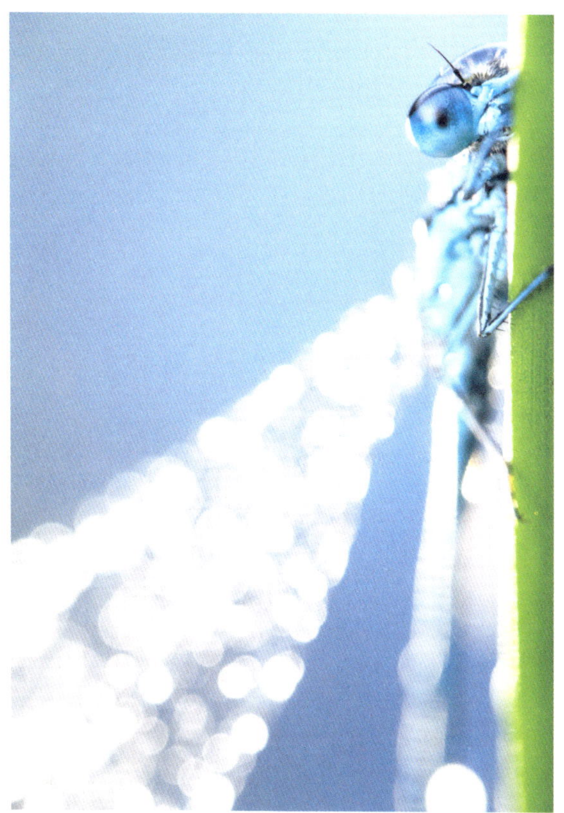

◀ *The main focal point—the damselfly's eye—is positioned too high and too far to the right in conventional terms, while most of the negative space is behind the subject. But the shot is successful—the image is more memorable because it breaks the rules.*

▼ *Having your subject exit the frame close to one edge, as the osprey does in this image, contradicts the normal rules of composition, but here it helps emphasize the bird's impact on the water.*

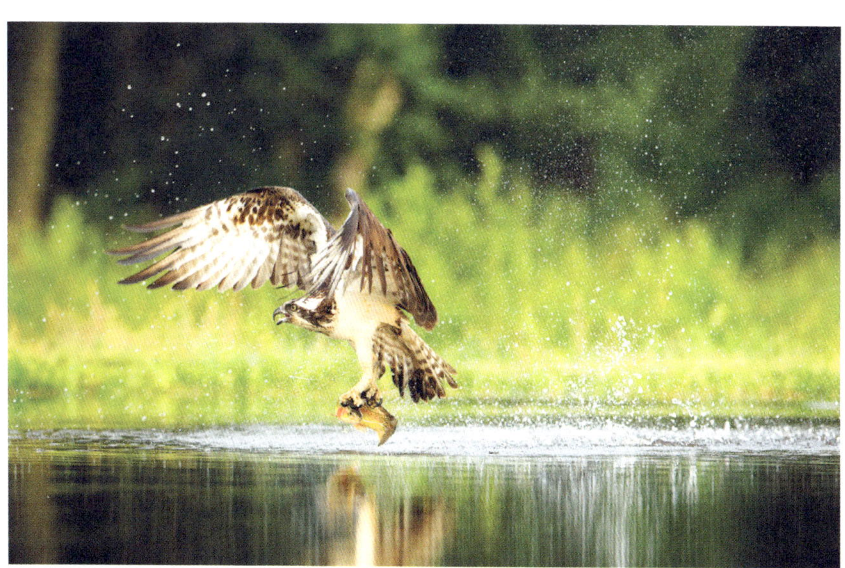

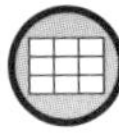

TECHNIQUE

- Include a frame, which can be natural or artificial, to imply depth and create interest.

- Your frame doesn't need to go around all four edges. A partial or incomplete frame is often just as effective.

- Trees, branches, foliage, a transition from light to shade, reeds, reflections, and cave openings are just some examples of the things you can use to frame the subject.

IN THE FRAME

Good compositions often possess balance as well as interest and a strong three-dimensional feel, and one way to create all this in an image is to include a "frame within a frame." And this is what we'd like you to do this time.

Much like a framed picture on a wall, using another object as a frame helps to separate the subject from the surrounding visual clutter and distraction. This places weight and emphasis on your focal point, creates layers within your shot, and gives the image an almost voyeuristic feel. It is an approach that can suit almost any type of subject. Nature provides a vast number of natural frames, some of which can be obvious, and others less so.

One way to create a frame is by using a secondary subject in the foreground. For example, consider using the body and legs of one animal to frame another behind, or use the stem or structure of foreground plants or flowers to create a frame for the bloom you are actually focused on. The frame will draw the eye further into the image, as well as provide context (information about how and where the subject lives).

To complete your assignment, set out to find three different ways of framing your subject, and use these to create three distinct images.

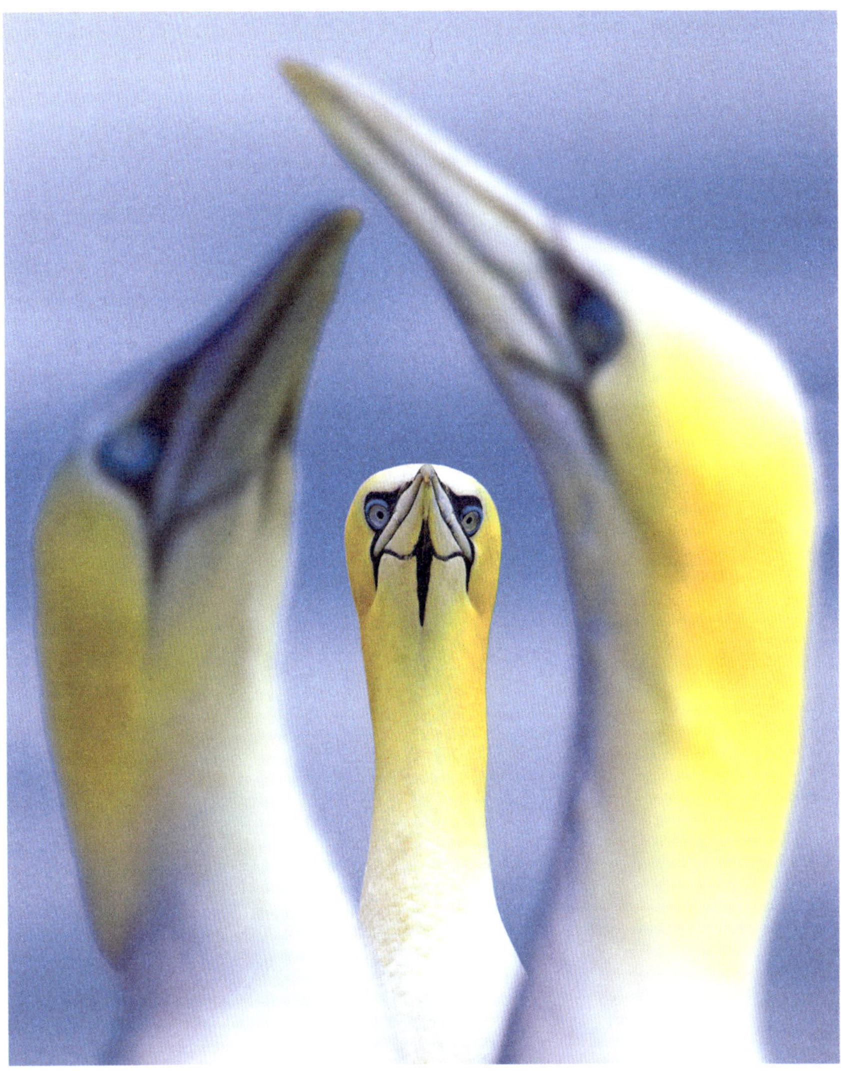

FIELD NOTES

- Using a shallow zone of focus can help create a frame.
  Grass and foliage–thrown out of focus by using a large
  aperture, long lens, or low viewpoint–can create what is
  sometimes referred to as a "dirty frame." Including
  bokeh in the foreground is another creative way to
  provide a soft frame for your main subject.

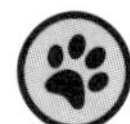
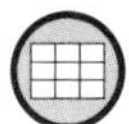

TECHNIQUE

- Only photograph subjects with strong, instantly recognizable outlines.

- Clean, simple backdrops, free of clutter or distraction, work best.

- Be careful when pointing your lens toward the sun or bright light. To minimize the risk of lens flare, attach a lens hood.

SPECTACULAR SILHOUETTES

For this assignment, we're asking you to photograph a silhouette. This is the most extreme form of backlighting (see page 24), in which the subject is recorded as an inky-black form, devoid of color or detail. Technically speaking, a silhouette is the result of gross underexposure, but, when combined with the right subject, the results can be bold and eye-catching, emphasizing shape and form.

To create a silhouette, your subject needs to be backlit or contrasted against a much brighter background, such as the sky. By shooting toward the brightness—sandwiching your subject between your camera and the light—you will render it as a silhouette. It is easiest to do this when the sun is low in the sky, so the early morning and late evening are good times for against-the-light, or "contre-jour," photography. Mist or water can also provide suitable backgrounds.

Your brief is to capture and print six images that show the natural world in silhouette. For each composition, think carefully about your shooting position and try to separate your subject from other elements within the frame. Avoid subjects that merge together, as these will appear as one ill-defined black blob. Shooting from a low angle, looking slightly upward, will help to project your subject clearly against its brighter background. Almost any animal or plant can work well in silhouette. Be imaginative and don't allow the pursuit of the "perfect exposure" to get in the way of a "creative exposure" that can achieve spectacular results.

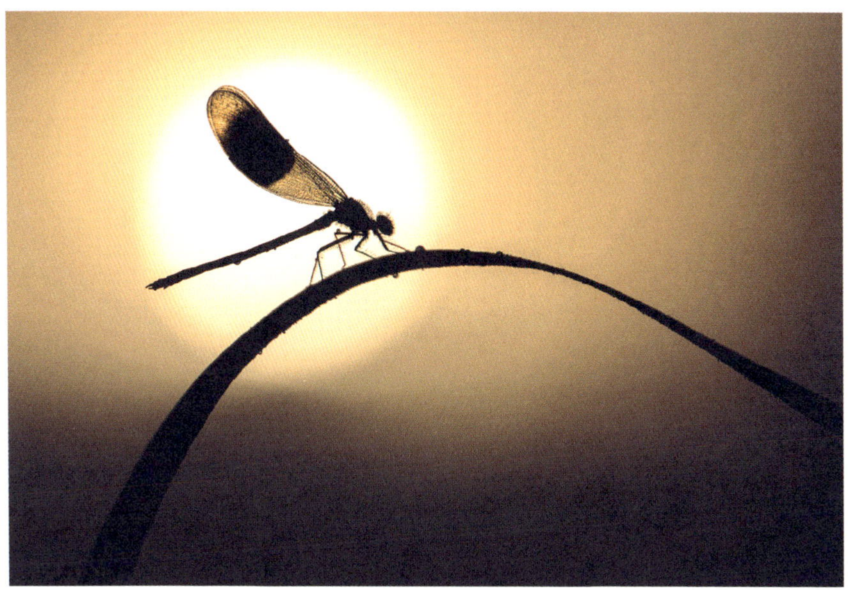

▲ *Light skies create the perfect contrast for shooting insect silhouettes.*

▼ *The "golden hours" are among the best times to shoot silhouettes. Colorful or dramatic skies contrast beautifully with inky-black foreground subjects.*

PRO TIPS

- Expect histograms to be skewed to the far left when shooting silhouettes. This illustrates that there are lots of dark or black tones within your shot.

- Don't rely on your camera's automatic exposure settings. Switch to spot metering mode and aim the metering point at the subject's brighter background to expose correctly for the background but lose detail in the subject. Alternatively, apply negative exposure compensation incrementally until you achieve the desired effect.

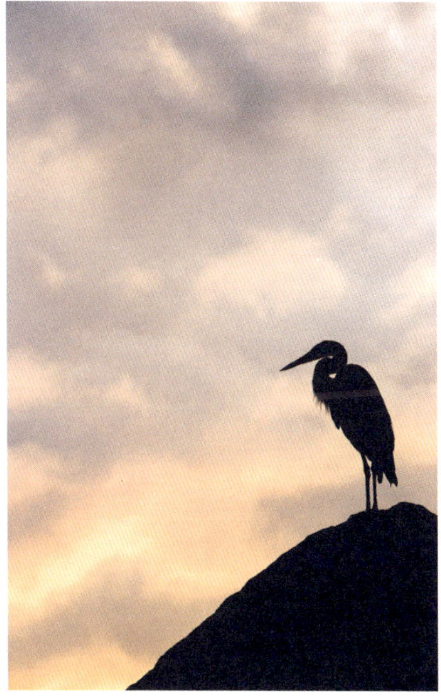

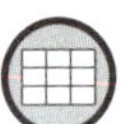
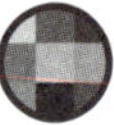

TECHNIQUE

- Arrive early and get into position before sunrise and at least one hour before sunset.

- Experiment with your orientation to the sun. Backlighting (see page 24) and sidelighting can produce dramatic results when the sun is low in the sky, emphasizing shapes and textures.

▼ *Due to the low contrast and warm light, dawn and dusk are great times to backlight your subject.*

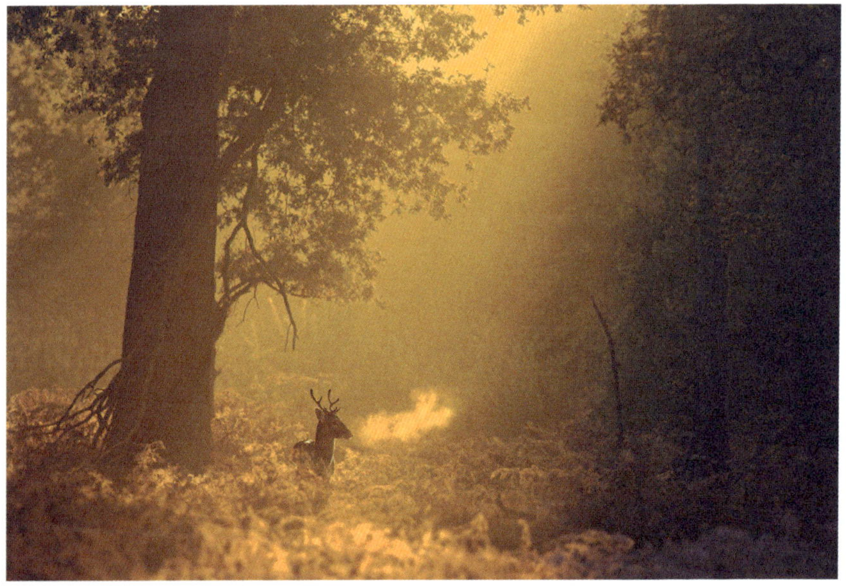

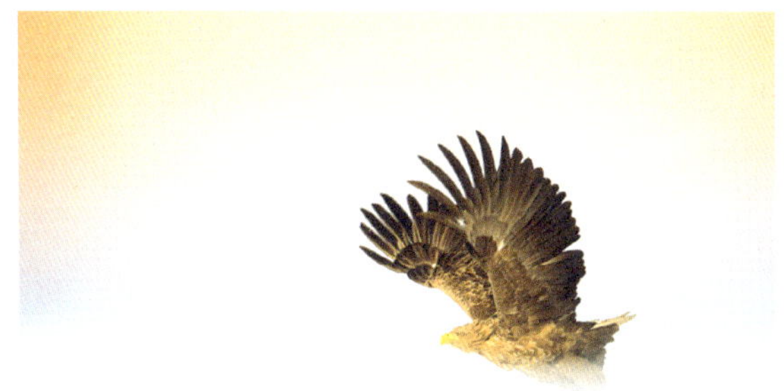

◄ The low angle of the sun at dawn and dusk can produce particularly beautiful colors. This image was taken just a few moments after sunrise, as a warm glow lit up the sky.

UP WITH THE LARK

This assignment requires you to set your alarm clock early: we want you to take a photograph at dawn. Shooting during what is known as the "golden hour" at sunrise, when the light is rich and warm, can be an effective way of creating atmosphere and capturing subtle detail that would otherwise be absent. The added advantage of shooting at dawn (and also dusk) is that most bird and animal species are more active, so there is no excuse for avoiding an early start.

When choosing a suitable location, avoid places that are overgrown and dense such as woodlands. Instead, pick a large, open area, such as grassland, moorland, or a large body of water—a lake or reservoir, perhaps. Arrive with plenty of time to spare, and then carefully assess the position of the rising sun.

Spend several mornings and evenings seeking out the best quality light to create a series of four images that highlight the beauty of the light during the golden hour.

FIELD NOTES

- Shooting towards the sun can cause exposure problems. Check your histogram regularly and use some exposure compensation if needed.

- Apps to help you predict the location of the sunrise in relation to your chosen viewpoint include PhotoPills and The Photographer's Ephemeris.

PRO TIPS

- Light temperature is measured in degrees Kelvin. When the sun is close to the horizon, the temperature of the light will measure between 1500 and 2500 degrees Kelvin. At these times, the wavelengths of the light are longer, creating a warm and rich glow, perfect for backlighting your subject.

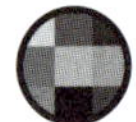
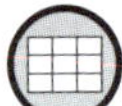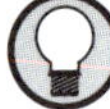

TECHNIQUE

- Shoot at a high ISO in low light. It is better to have to reduce the resulting noise in post-processing than shoot a soft image that cannot be improved later.

- On dark, overcast days, the light will often lack contrast and mean your camera's autofocus system will struggle. Switch to manual focus for consistent results.

- A fast shutter speed will freeze the motion of rain droplets or snowflakes, while a slow shutter speed will render them as streaks.

- Snow will fool a camera into underexposing, so dial in plenty of positive exposure compensation and check the histogram.

- Invest in a waterproof cover to protect both your camera and lens.

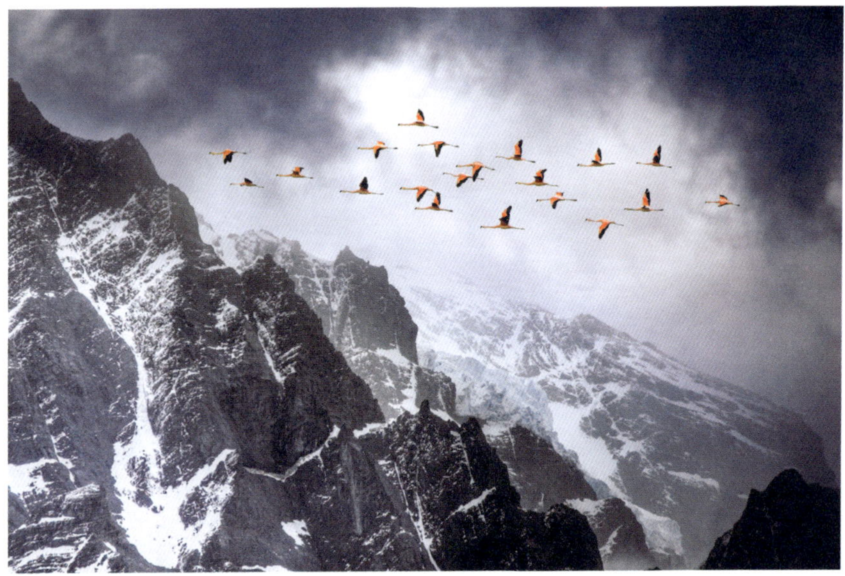

▲ *The dark sky in this image helps to give a sense of atmosphere. The weather, the mountainous environment in the background, and the delicate birds all combine to tell a story.*

PERFECT STORM

Many effective images are taken in extreme weather conditions. Falling snow, stormy skies, churning seas, and even rain can add an extra element to an image that tells a story and draws the viewer into the subject's world. Your brief here is to make the most of adverse weather, and to do that you must know how to best exploit it.

Snow, for instance, can be used to create a feeling of exposure and extremity. Try heading into the hills to capture subjects against an expansive and desolate landscape. Give the subject space in the frame to accentuate the element of weather. This, in turn, can lead to a feeling of solitude, adding power and feeling to your images. Stormy weather and high winds can churn up the sea, creating a real sense of wildness—the perfect scenario for capturing seabirds in flight. Rain, too, can add its own special type of atmosphere. When shooting in either light or heavy rain, background choice becomes important. A dark background will make the rain appear more prominent, so look for areas of shadow to shoot toward.

So the next time it rains, get your waterproofs on, go out and begin this project. Over time, collect four of your best images showing wildlife battling the elements.

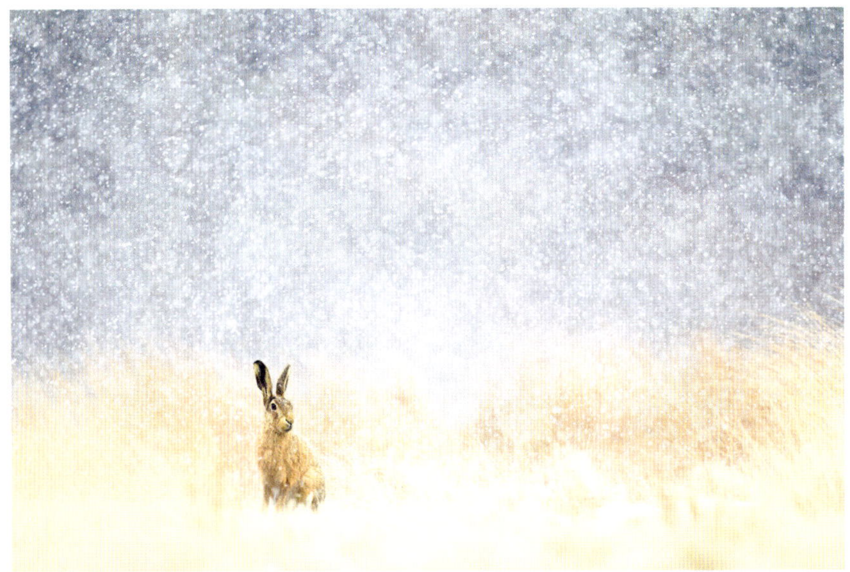

▲ *A fast shutter speed will freeze falling snowflakes as white spots mid-air.*

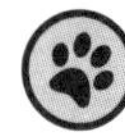

TECHNIQUE

- When setting out to capture wildlife in each season, look for locations and subjects that are easy to access and offer lots of potential images.

- Food will often grow scarcer in the winter months, forcing subjects to be bolder and making them easier to approach. This is a great time of year to set up a feeding station (see page 14).

- Spring blossom and fall foliage are photogenic subjects in their own right but they also provide colorful, seasonal backgrounds to animals, birds, and insects.

SEASON BY SEASON

For this project, we want you to capture four related images, each illustrating an aspect of nature in one season. For example, you may decide to photograph the same subject at different times of the year in seasonal settings. For subjects that you don't see throughout the year, such as insects and reptiles, adapt the theme. For example, try photographing them through the stages of their life instead.

There are many different subjects and approaches that each season presents. During spring, you can set out to capture the birds that are breeding, young animals with their parents, and reptiles emerging from their winter slumber. The summer is a great time of year to focus on butterflies and dragonflies, and many habitats burst into colorful life with photogenic wildflowers. Foliage turns golden in the fall, when birds and animals feast on berries and natural fruits, and deer enter the rutting season. Mist, fog, frost, and snow can provide atmospheric and photogenic conditions during the winter. This is also the best time of year to capture species battling against the elements, or new species that have migrated to escape colder climates.

However you decide to approach this assignment, take your time and feel free to be creative, but the aim is to produce four photographs that tell a seasonal story.

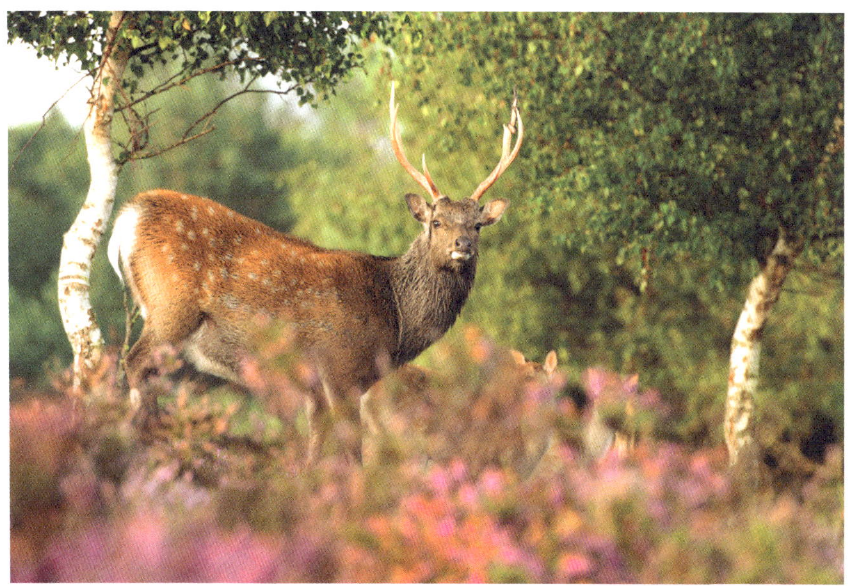

▲ *Capture your subject through the seasons. Here, flowering heather conveys a feeling of summer.*

▼ *This almost monochrome image of the dark deer against the pale snow evokes the cold winter months.*

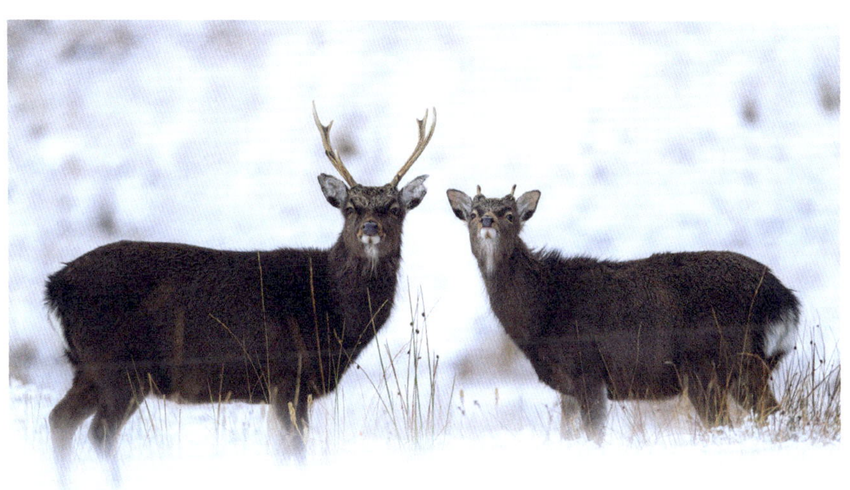

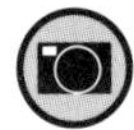
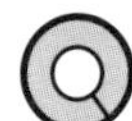
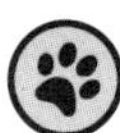
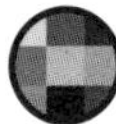

TECHNIQUE

- You will need to make a reflector for this assignment to help you bounce light onto small subjects such as plants and butterflies.

- Unlike using flash, you can preview and fine-tune the effect of reflected light on your subject before pressing the shutter.

- Either ask someone to help you by holding the reflector while you work your camera, or use a clamp to hold the disc in position.

REFLECT THE LIGHT

Light is often in short supply when shooting close-ups of invertebrates and plant life, but you can remedy this by using a small reflector, and this assignment is all about learning to use one creatively.

A reflector is a "must-have" accessory for any nature photographer—it is a white disc that is positioned close to your subject in order to bounce light onto it. This "lifts" your subject by providing extra illumination while banishing ugly shadow areas. Ideally, the subject needs to be stationary, so photography with a reflector is best suited to flowers, fungi, and roosting, dormant insects.

Although small reflectors aren't particularly expensive, to complete this assignment we actually want you to make your own and then use it to capture some beautifully lit close-ups. Just wrap some kitchen foil over a piece of cardboard, about 12 x 8in (30 x 20cm) in diameter. You could even just use a piece of stiff white card or a mirror. All are good budget options. Now, head out with your camera and shoot three comparison sets—of different subjects—showing the effects with and without reflected light. Play with the angle and proximity of the reflector to create different results.

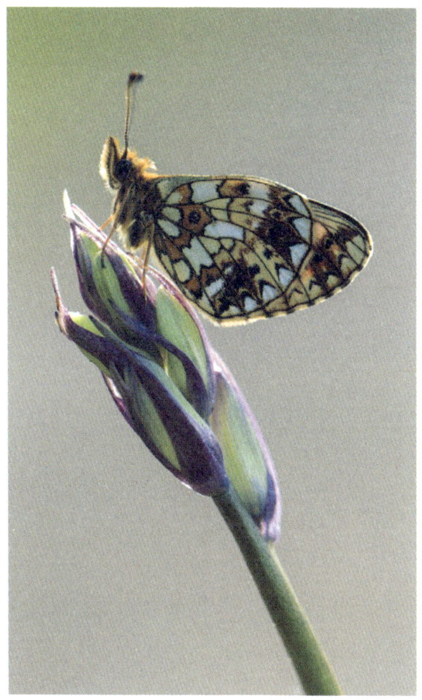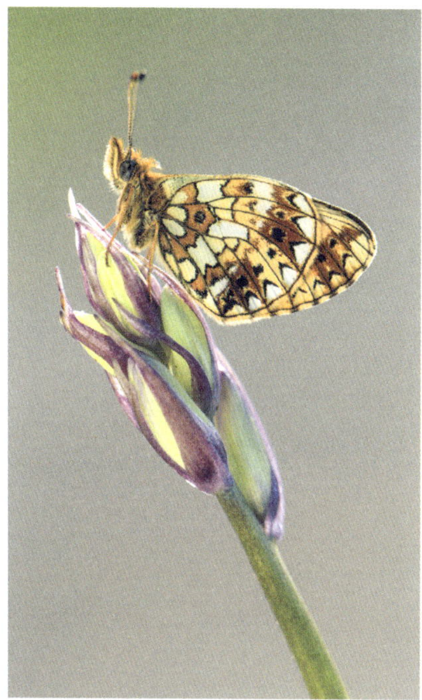

▲ *Once you see the dramatic difference that using a reflector (right) makes compared to not using one (left), you will never be without one again.*

PRO TIPS

• The reflector's color is important. A pure white reflector provides soft, diffused light. Silver is more efficient, but the light it produces is harsher, while a gold disc will add warmth to reflected light. Some reflectors have a different color on either side.

• You can alter the intensity of reflected light by moving the disc closer to or further away from your subject, or changing the disc's angle. Lastolite are among the leading makers of reflectors, which are often collapsible so they can be carried easily.

ASSIGNMENT JOURNAL

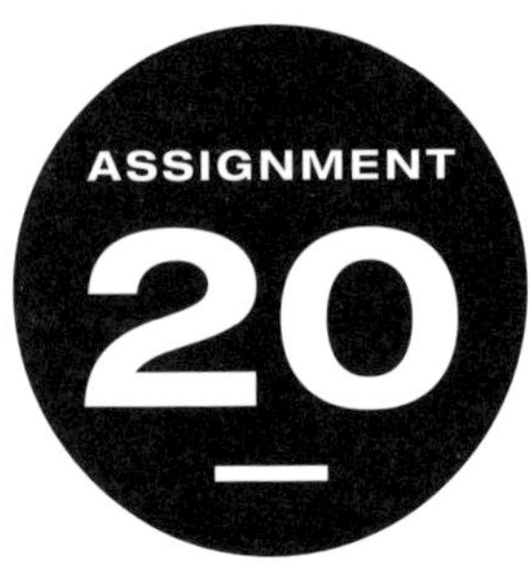

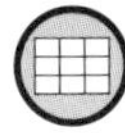

TECHNIQUE

- Learn to habitually explore the background of your image so you can identify and eliminate any distractions.

- Selecting a larger aperture creates a shallower zone of focus and reduces the impact of background elements.

- If there is no way to avoid background distractions, crop in tightly to your subject to exclude them.

- Photographing sunlit subjects against a shady background can highlight your subject's color and detail against a striking black backdrop.

BEAUTIFUL BACKGROUNDS

A background has the power to make or break an image, which is why we want you to create four images of different subjects—plant, insect, animal, and bird—while paying special attention to your backdrops.

Ugly background elements, such as distracting grasses, branches, vegetation, artificial objects, or highlights, will weaken or even ruin your photographs. Except when you wish to capture your subject in its environment (see page 32), you will need to isolate it against a clean, diffused, colorful, or complementary background. In order to do this, you might have to alter your perspective, shooting position, or focal length, or wait for the subject to move into a better position. Sometimes, you will only need to move a few inches to the left or right, or up or down, to exclude that annoying branch, fence post, or stump from your subject's background. But doing so can make all the difference.

When shooting wildlife, it is easy to be so focused on your subject that you don't spot distractions elsewhere in the frame until you later download your shots. But this project will teach you to avoid this type of error and prevent disappointment.

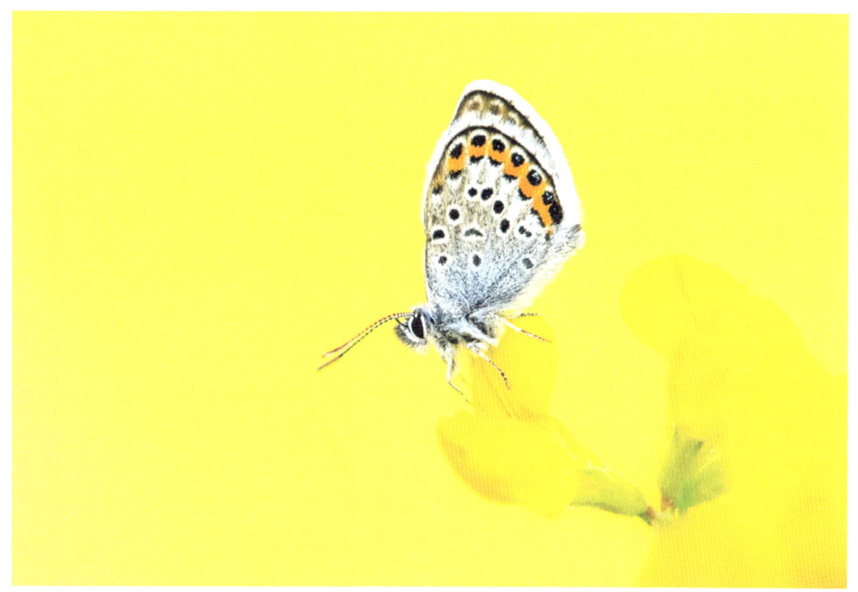

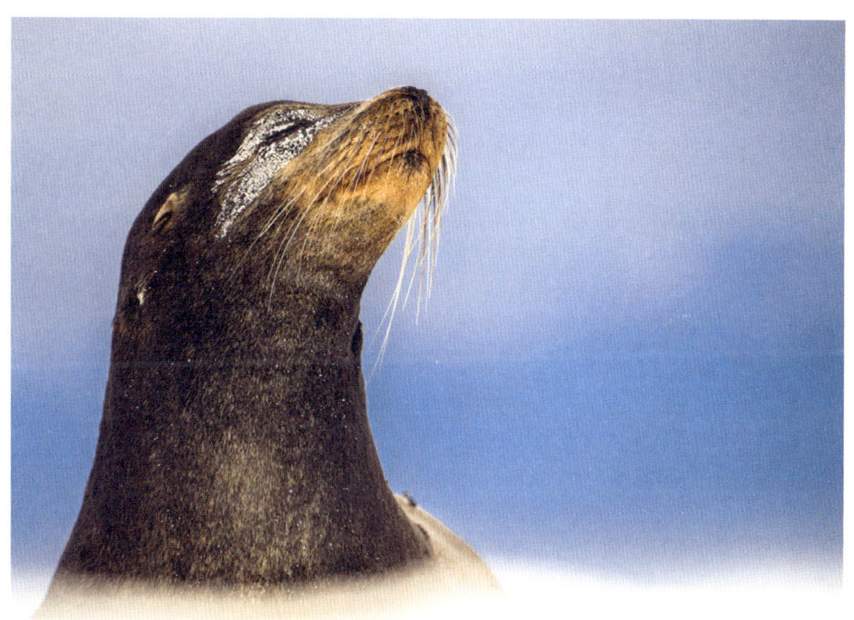

▲ This bright, impactful yellow backdrop is 100 percent natural, created by shooting the butterfly against background vegetation which has been lit up by golden evening light.

▼ Sky and water will normally provide a natural, colorful, and uniform backdrop for animal portraits, free of distractions.

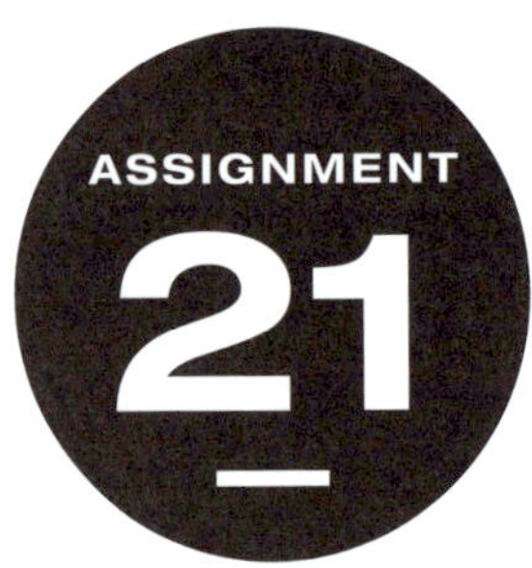

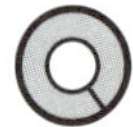
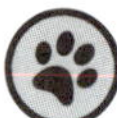
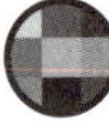

TECHNIQUE

- When positioning the light, always keep it just out of frame, being careful not to create flare.

- You can alter the light's intensity by simply moving the device closer or further away.

▼ *These three images were taken just moments apart, but are dramatically different because of the lighting. The first picture was taken using natural light; the second with a camera-mounted LED device to create front lighting; and the third while holding the LED behind the butterfly to mimic natural backlighting.*

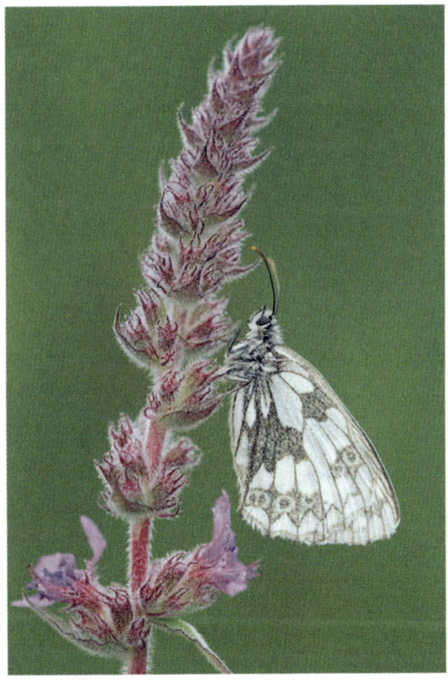

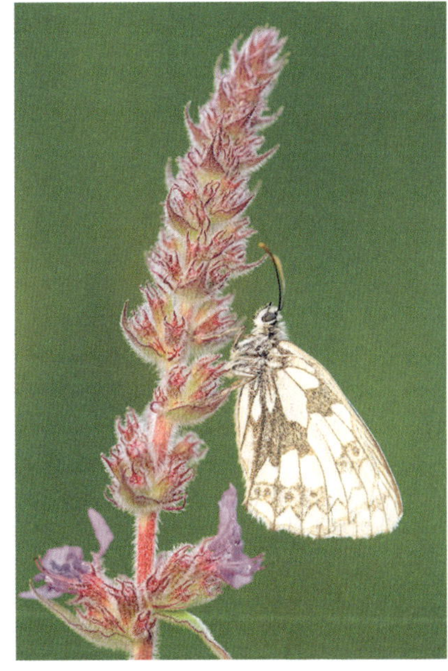

A BUG'S LIGHT

When photographing small subjects, such as insects, fungi, or flowers, it is relatively easy to alter and enhance the light for corrective or creative purposes. In this project, we'll be asking you to take a series of close-up shots of insects, while holding an LED light in different positions. Embrace all the creative possibilities that manipulating light can bring—learning to use light will greatly improve your nature close-ups. Once you have some images, study the results.

Flash is likely to frighten skittish subjects away, so it's best to use a continuous light source. While a reflector (see page 48) can be useful, it doesn't allow you to generate light from any angle or vary its intensity, unlike a small LED light. Although an LED device can't match the power of a burst of flash, it provides a continuous light source, which is far easier to work with—you can constantly see its effect, and preview the results. Hold the light in your hand and slowly move it around your subject. Positioning the light behind an insect, for example, will create backlighting that will enhance translucent insect wings and highlight tiny details.

However, your subject ideally needs to be inanimate. Only photograph a roosting butterfly in the early morning or late evening when the insect is cool and inactive, or look for a snail or ladybird in your garden. Complete this assignment by printing three of your favorite and most creative photographs.

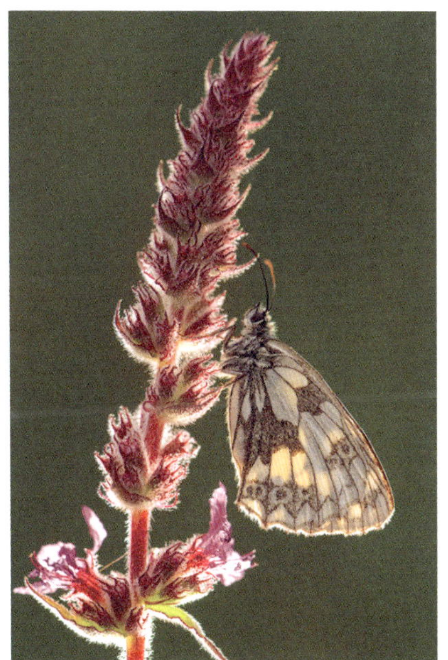

PRO TIPS

- You don't need a large or costly LED device for this project—you could use the flashlight on your smartphone, or a cheap, standard LED light from a hardware store. However, a dedicated device for photography—such as a Manfrotto LUMIMUSE or Rotolight NEO—will provide more functionality, power, and control over the light's color temperature.

- You can also try altering the light's color by placing colored acetate gels over the light.

- Strong natural light will overwhelm LED lights. Their effect will be most pronounced in overcast conditions.

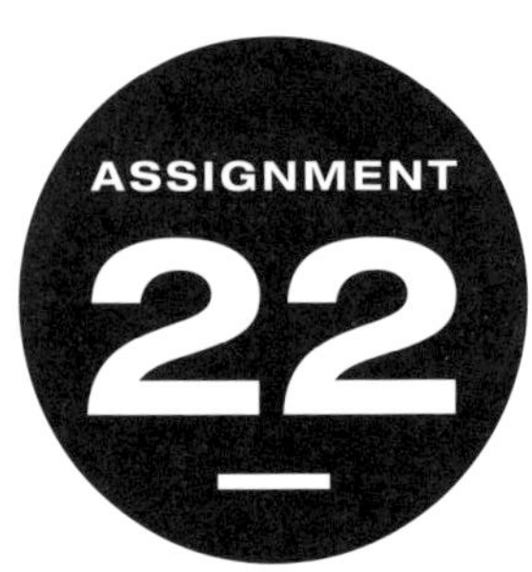

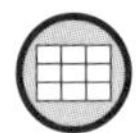
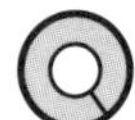
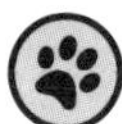

TECHNIQUE

- Use a 300mm telephoto lens or longer to isolate plumage and feather detail.

- Fill the frame for impact.

- For butterflies and dragonflies, use a close-up attachment (see page 20).

- You can use an extension tube to enable the lens to focus more closely, or a teleconverter to increase its magnification.

- Opt for a small aperture (f/11 to f/18) to keep insect wings pin-sharp, or select a large aperture (f/2.8 or f/4) to create artistic images, with a shallow zone of focus.

SPREAD YOUR WINGS

Your brief here is to look very closely at a bird's feathers or the patterns on a butterfly's or dragonfly's wing, and to photograph a series of close-ups of the extraordinary and beautiful details you find.

Your biggest challenge is getting close enough to fill the frame with the wings and feathers alone. Wild birds are unlikely to allow you to approach near enough to capture close-up studies of plumage. Instead, visit a location where subjects are already accustomed to human contact and allow you to approach closely, such as a wetlands reserve, local park, or canal. Semi-tame birds, such as geese, swans, or ducks, will often tolerate you getting within just a few yards. Ignore conventional shots and use a telephoto lens to explore the beauty of their wings. Soft, overcast light will help you to capture fine, exquisite details. You can also look for moulted feathers lying on the ground, which you can photograph in the comfort of your home. And don't overlook the potential of smaller winged creatures—butterflies and dragonflies also have intricately patterned wings. Use a macro lens to isolate color, detail, or dewy wingtips.

Once you have assembled a series of photographs of wing and feather details, create a montage of your best six images to showcase nature's wonderful patterns and your own creative vision.

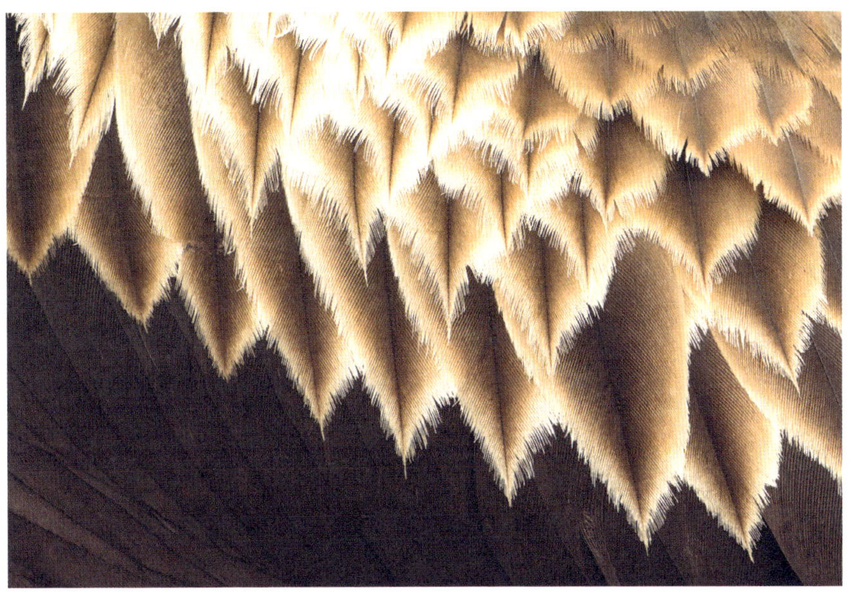

▲ *The exquisite detail and contrast of this frigate bird's plumage justified the tight crop.*

▼ *You don't always have to capture your subject in its entirety. A more creative approach can sometimes convey far more about the subject, including awe and wonder at its beauty.*

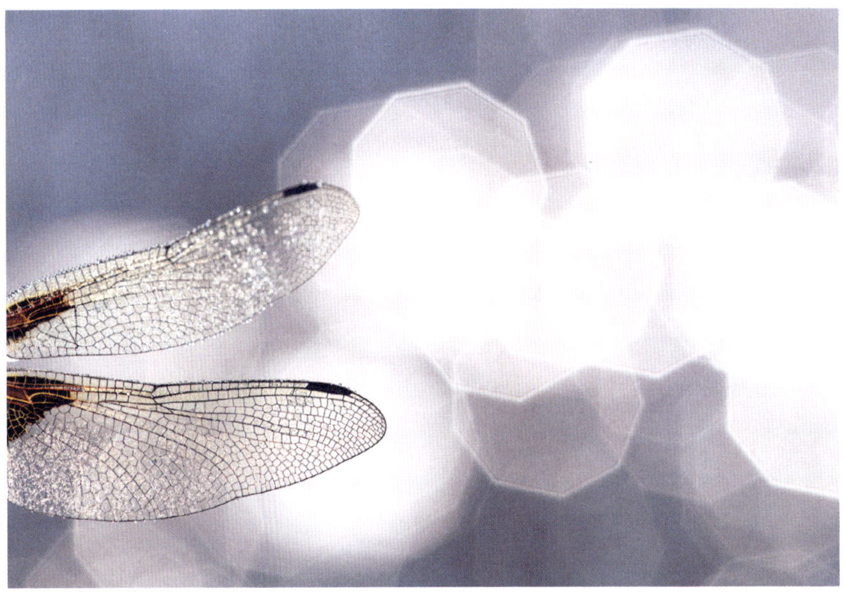

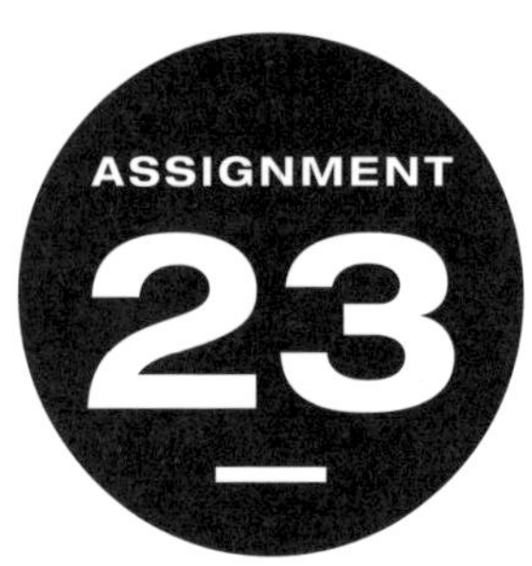

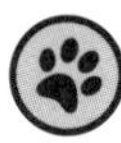

TECHNIQUE

- Use waterproof wood stain to protect your blind from the elements.

- Cut out a low window to enable you to get to eye level with subjects on the ground.

- You are likely to be in your hide for long periods of time so comfort should be a priority. Investing in a good-quality fishing chair will be money well spent.

HIDE AND SEEK

Most wildlife is shy, so photographing it from a blind (also known as a hide) is often the only way to get close enough, even when using long telephoto lenses. There are plenty of purpose-built blinds you can buy online, but these can be expensive. For this assignment, you'll be building your own simple blind, which will be much cheaper and just as effective.

A blind is most productive when used near a feeding station, roosting site, or breeding ground, or any other area your subject is likely to return to regularly. Since it is likely to attract unwanted human attention, it is best to find a spot for it on private land. Ask the permission of a local landowner, perhaps in return for some free prints of the images you take. Farmland attracts lots of animals and a variety of bird species. Avoid open ground, instead looking for locations by hedgerows or other convenient foliage that will break up the blind's shape and help it to better resemble part of the landscape. Ideally, you should leave your blind in place for as long as possible to allow the local wildlife to grow accustomed to it.

The assignment continues on pages 58–9 with instructions on how to make a basic blind. Once you're set up, take your time to develop a portfolio of close-up shots of wildlife, and use the blind to complete some of the other assignments in this book.

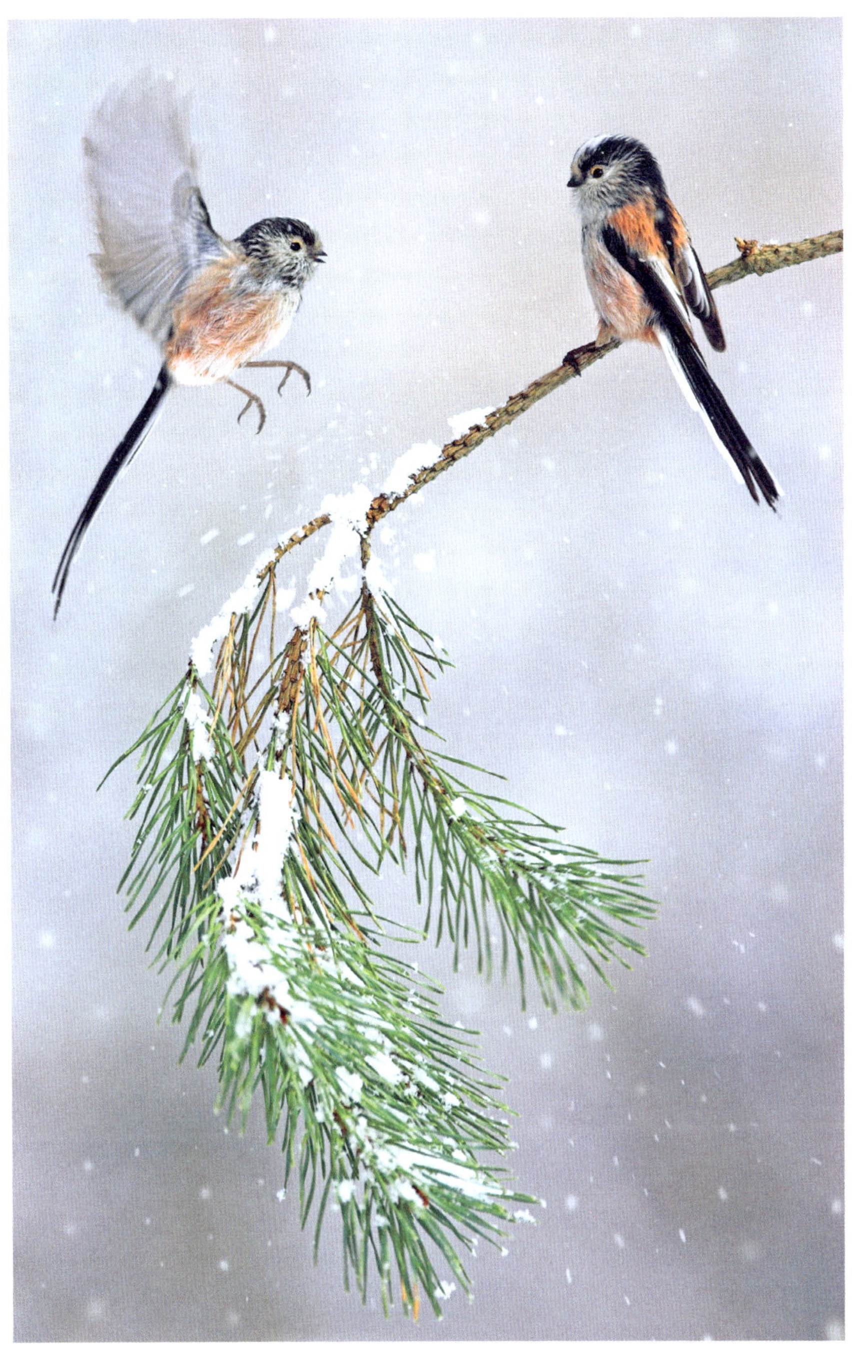

▲ *Building a blind in your garden can be a great way of getting close to garden birds.*

BUILD YOUR OWN BLIND

Building a blind, or hide, is much easier than you might imagine. Once you've identified the right location, such as your back garden, you can make a start with these basic instructions:

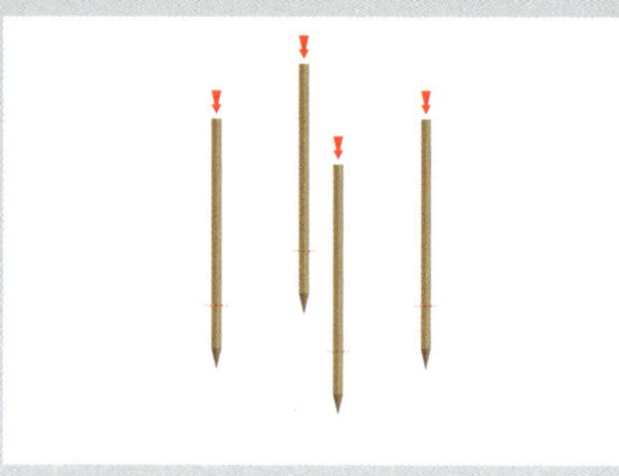

1 Start by hammering four stakes into the ground at each corner.

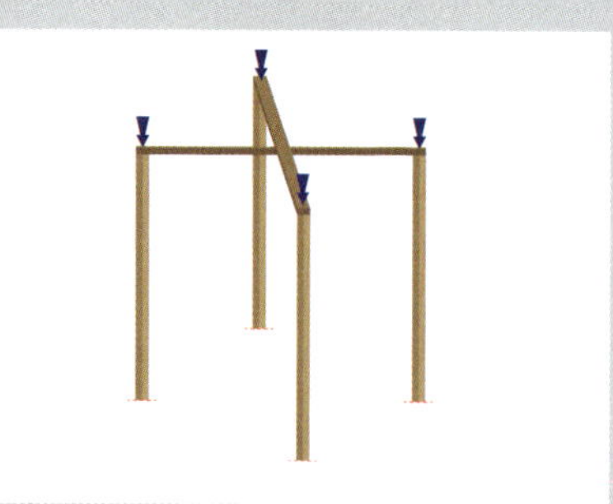

2 Place two wooden slats across the top to form a cross, screwing each end into the top of the stake.

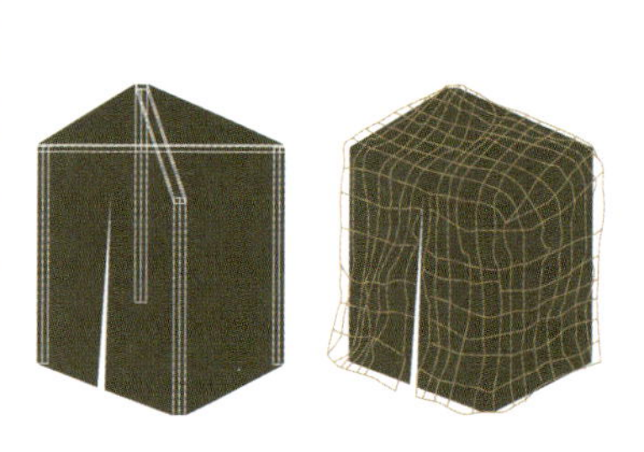

3 Drape a waterproof tarpaulin over the frame, then cover it with camouflaged scrim netting. Cut a slit at the back to allow you to enter and exit.

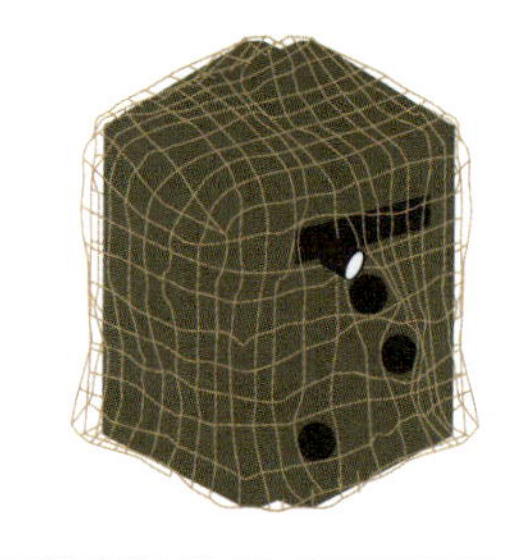

4 Cut out windows at suitable heights for your lens. Also make a viewing slot to allow you to observe the wildlife comfortably.

FIELD NOTES

- You can place a camera trap at the blind to record wildlife activity when you are not there. This can provide vital help in planning the most productive times to visit.

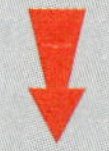

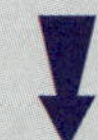

BUILD A FLOATING BLIND

A floating blind is a great way to get close to waterbirds. It also provides a low angle of view so you can photograph birds at their eye level, giving your images intimacy and impact.

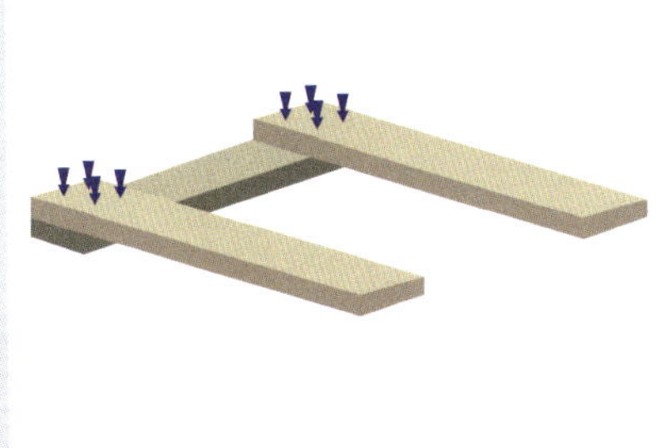

1 Screw three planks of wood together to form a U-shape.

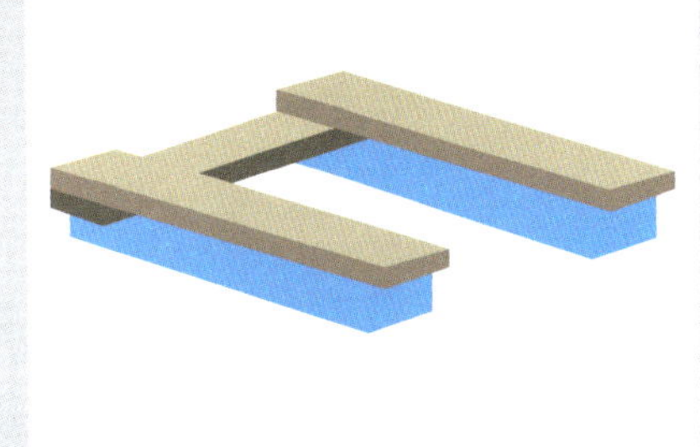

2 Attach three large blocks of polystyrene to the bottom of the planks using wood glue or PVA. These create enough buoyancy for the blind to float while supporting your camera and a large lens.

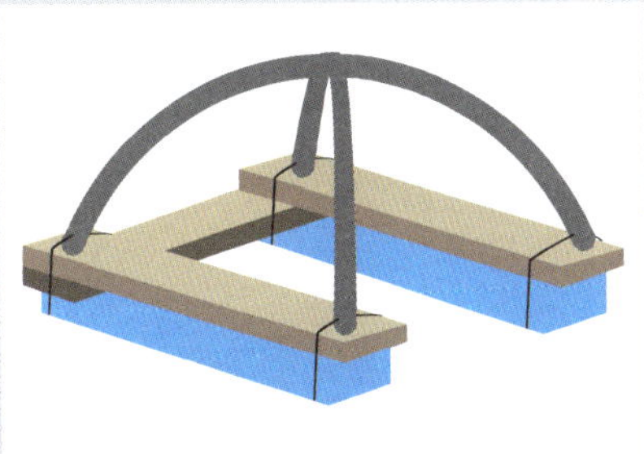

3 Bend two plastic plumbing pipes from corner to corner, across each other, to form a frame that will support the canopy. Attach by piercing the tubes, threading through zip ties, and tying these around the floats.

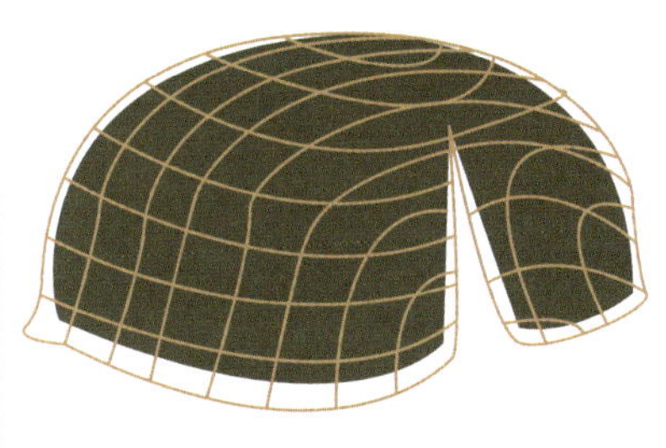

4 Drape a waterproof tarpaulin completely over the frame to form the roof, and then cover it with camouflaged scrim netting. Cut a slit at the back of the tarpaulin and netting to allow you to enter.

5 Wear neoprene waders to wade into the water, while holding the floating frame over you. Take care not to go too deep or where there might be underwater hazards.

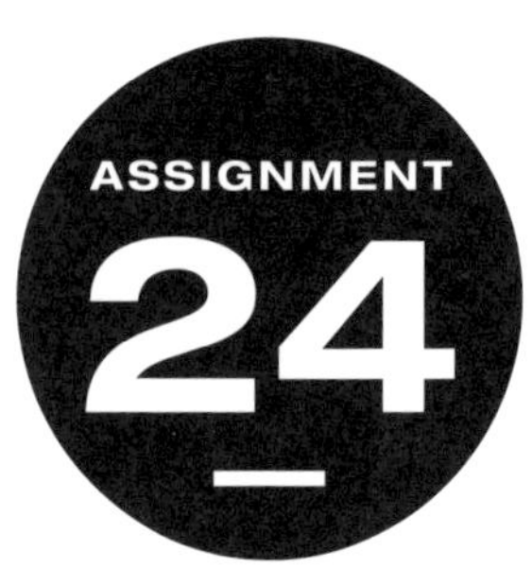

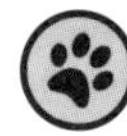

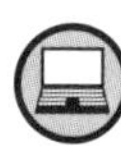

TECHNIQUE

- Research your subject thoroughly. The more you know about it, the greater chance you have of capturing special images.

- Although plenty of information is available online, search your local library for specialist nature books that contain critical information about your subject.

- As well as showing behavior, vary your compositions creatively using different weather and light conditions.

SPECIES STUDY

One of the most important aspects of wildlife photography is developing an understanding of your subject. Here, we are asking you to get to know a single species, observe its behavior carefully, and then photograph it over time to create a series of images that represent its life cycle.

Learn as much as you possibly can about your chosen subject. Look at the typical habitat that it can be found in, the time of day when it is most active, its feeding and breeding habits, and any other information you can find. This knowledge will save you countless hours in the field. Once you have researched your subject thoroughly, the next step is to find a suitable site and visit it regularly throughout the year, recording behavioral patterns. Don't forget to consider the light—for example, where is the sun when your subject is most active? Make a note of how can you orientate yourself for the most dramatic lighting and effective backgrounds.

Understanding a subject in depth will give you a greater chance of creating successful images that tell a story and give a real insight into a species. The assignment continues on pages 62–3 with tips on how to choose your subject.

▲ *Knowledge of both the location and behavior of this mountain hare was vital in capturing an intimate portrait. There are no shortcuts—understanding a species takes time.*

▼ *This image of two red deer stags was captured after years returning to the same location, observing behavior and light. Patience and perseverance were key.*

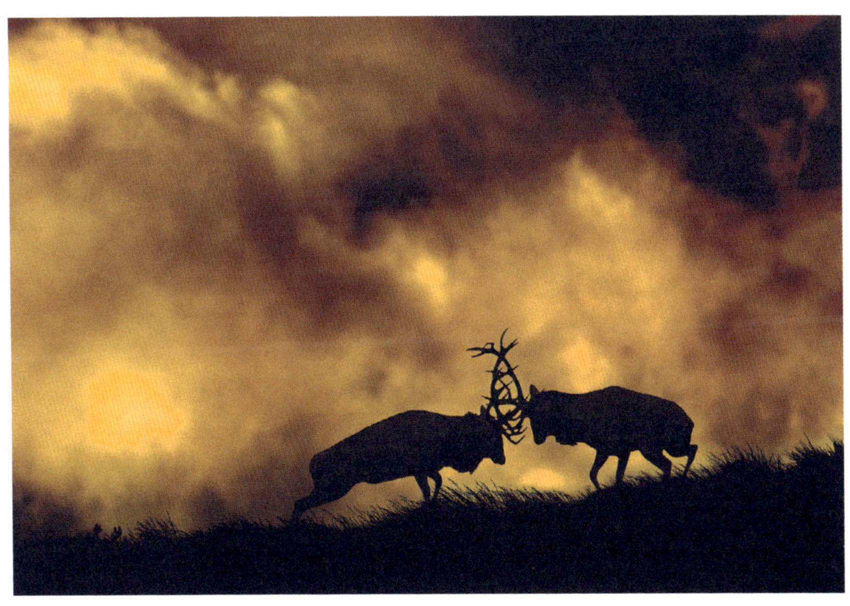

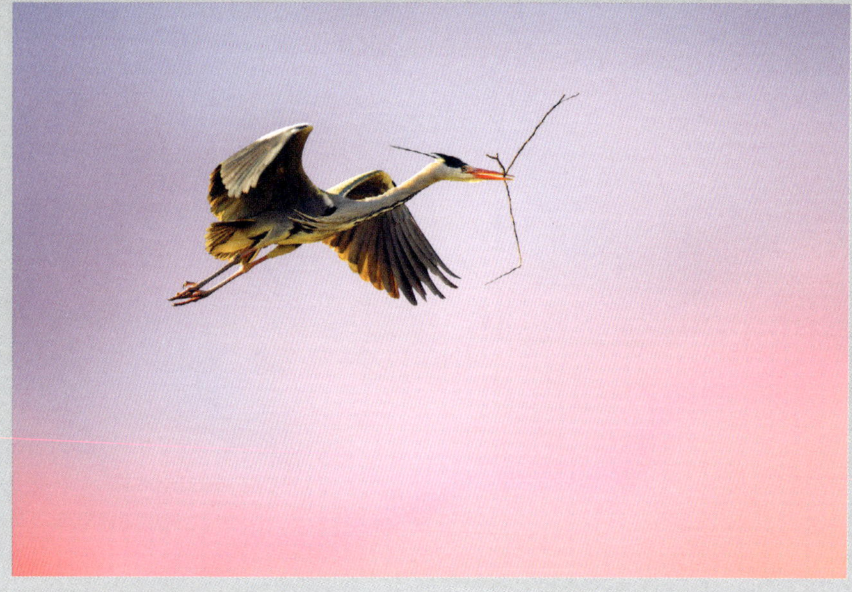

▲ *During early spring (or even late winter, as in the case of this gray heron) birds will start building nests, offering an array of photographic opportunities.*

SELECT A SPECIES

It is important to select your subject carefully. Think about accessibility and distance—it's much better to stick to a local habitat so you can use your time productively.

• You will need to visit frequently, at different times of the year, to build up an understanding of the species and shoot a strong series of images.

• Think carefully about the pictures that may be possible and try to visualize them in your mind.

• Birds are particularly well suited to this assignment, as they can be photographed at different developmental stages through the seasons, allowing you to study courtship, singing, nest-building, feeding, and fledging. Bear in mind that you may need a licence to photograph some rarer species at a nest (see page 111).

• During early spring, aim to capture behavioral shots of animals and birds depicting courtship and territorial displays.

• Young are usually born in late spring or summer, so this is the perfect time to capture tender images of a mother feeding.

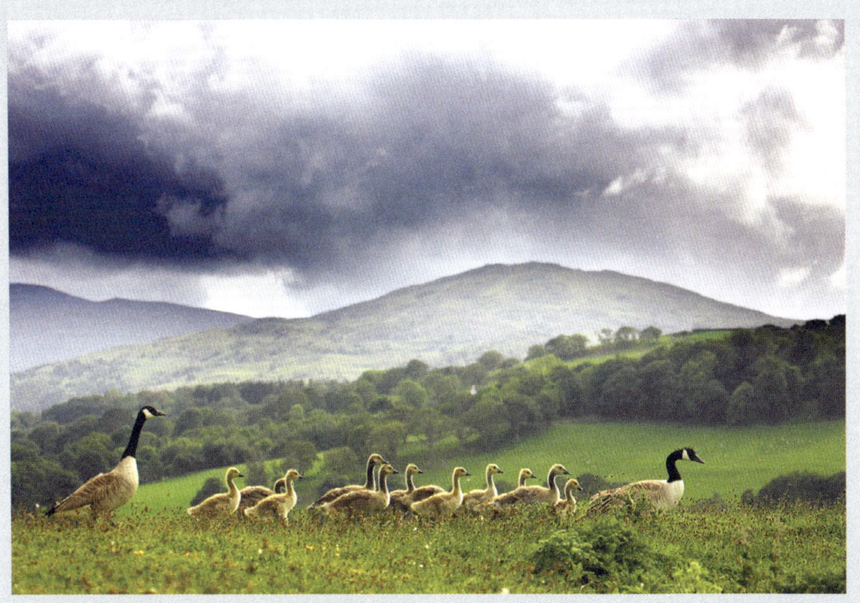

▲ *This image of a family of Canada geese depicts the concept of family unity and balance.*

ASSIGNMENT JOURNAL

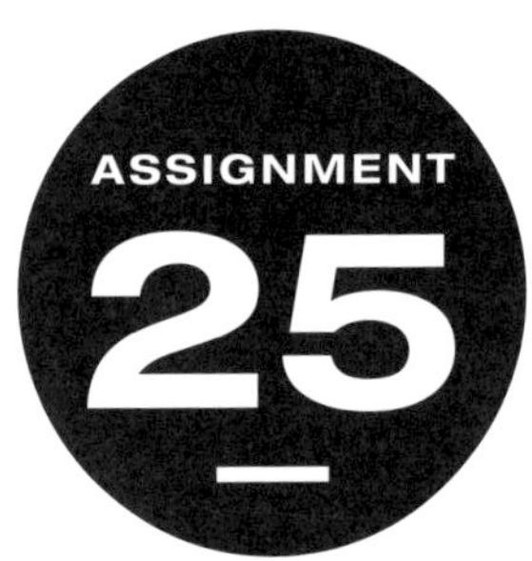

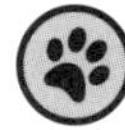

TECHNIQUE

- Keep your stalking outfit unwashed. The fresh smell of washing powder will be a sure giveaway.

- When beginning a stalk, it is impossible to know how close you will get. Take some "insurance" images along the way. If your subject bolts, you will at least have something to show for your efforts.

- Don't set your sights too high at first. Choose a subject that is accessible and will allow you multiple attempts.

FIELDCRAFT

In order to be a successful wildlife photographer, you should not only understand the behavior of your subject, but learn the fieldcraft skills, such as stalking technique, required to approach it. For this assignment, we would like you to practice stalking a species, seeing how near you can approach it before it runs or flies away. Then print your best, closest photograph captured in this way.

Stalking can be frustrating and time-consuming, but it is sometimes the only way to photograph a subject up close. Avoid wearing bright colors—muted greens and browns help you blend into the environment. Full camouflage gear is only necessary for the most sensitive species. Make sure the fabric is silent when you move—most animals have much better hearing than us. Before beginning your stalk, plan out your approach. Look for elements in the landscape you can use to conceal your presence, and keep downwind so your subject doesn't pick up your scent.

Finally, be aware of your subject at all times and watch for signs of unease. If the animal suddenly looks alert, freeze, and don't move again until it has settled. Learning to "read" your subject and understanding when your actions would be unethical (see page 111) are important parts of fieldcraft.

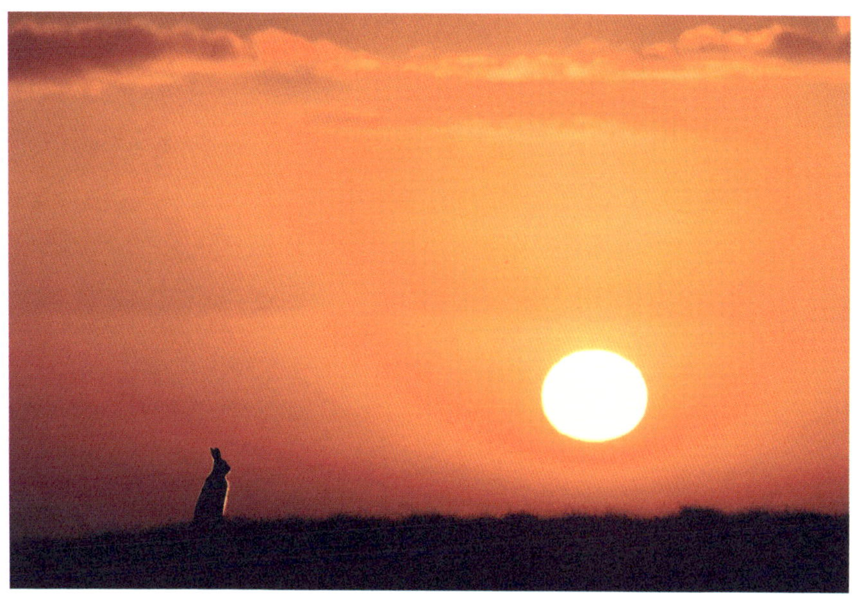

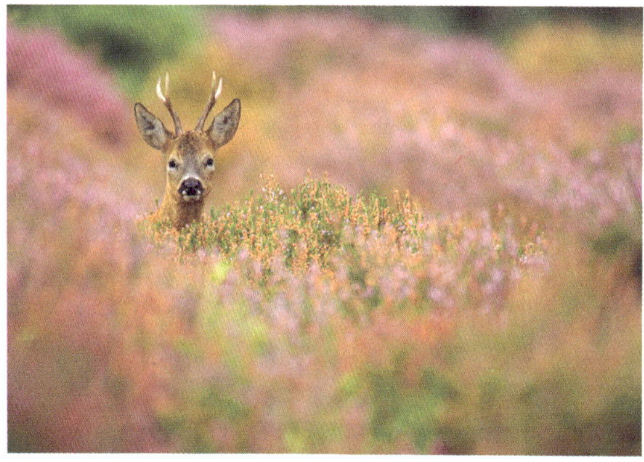

▲ Getting close enough to capture the silhouette of this mountain hare against the setting sun required a slow and steady approach.

◄ Sometimes, the best images are captured at the moment the subject is alerted and eye contact is made, so make sure you keep your camera ready to shoot at all times, but be careful not to cause the animal any distress.

FIELD NOTES

- It is important to travel light when stalking. Take just one camera body and one lens. For support, avoid using a tripod as they can be too cumbersome–opt for a monopod or a beanbag for low-level subjects.

- Stay low and keep your profile below the horizon at all times. If your silhouette is visible against the sky, you will alert your subject.

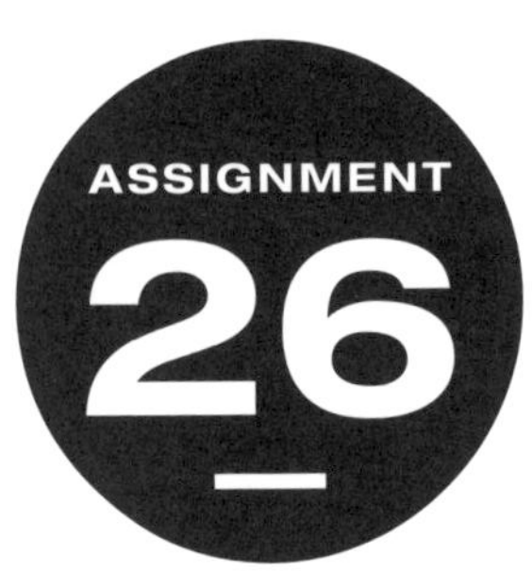

 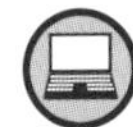
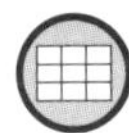 

TECHNIQUE

- Select your subjects and compositions for your black-and-white images by concentrating on contrast, texture, shape, and form.

- Shoot in color to capture the largest tonal range and then convert the files to black and white in post-processing on the computer.

NATURE IN BLACK AND WHITE

The natural world is so vibrant that it might seem counterintuitive to think of it in black and white, but monochrome or "mono" images can convey mood, drama, and emotion in a unique way. When creating a black-and-white image, however, you remove the impact as well as the distraction of color. So, for this assignment you will need to rely more heavily on contrast, light, texture, shape, and form for your photographs to really stand out. Again, keeping it simple will often create the most striking images.

Think carefully about subject selection. Not all images will benefit from color being removed. Many nature photographs require color for impact, subject identification, and to provide context. Ideally, you should be shooting specifically for mono, previsualizing your images in black and white before pressing the shutter. It shouldn't be an afterthought—converting to mono can't disguise a poor image.

Harsh midday sunlight can suit mono, as can overcast conditions—low-contrast light helps you record the texture and detail of fur, skin, and plumage. Subjects photographed against light (such as silhouettes, see page 40) or dark backdrops naturally suit black-and-white treatment. Also look for natural patterns and repetition.

So, to complete this assignment, we want you to shoot a series of eight varied photographs with the intention of capturing nature in black and white, fine-art style.

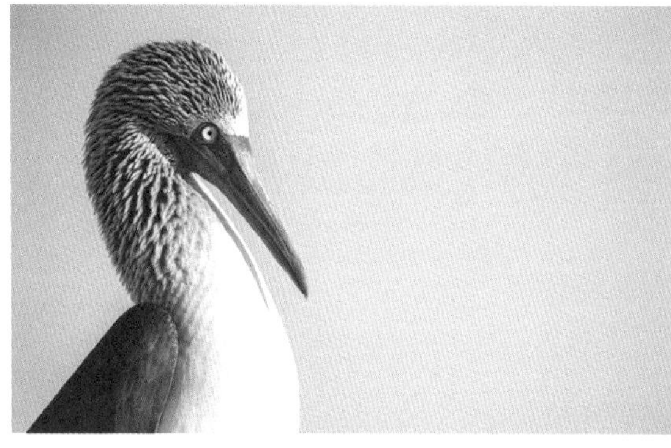

◄ *Bold and simple compositions often work best. The detailed textures of fur, skin, and plumage can look extraordinary in black and white.*

▼ *Any wildlife subject, big or small, can be suitable for mono treatment.*

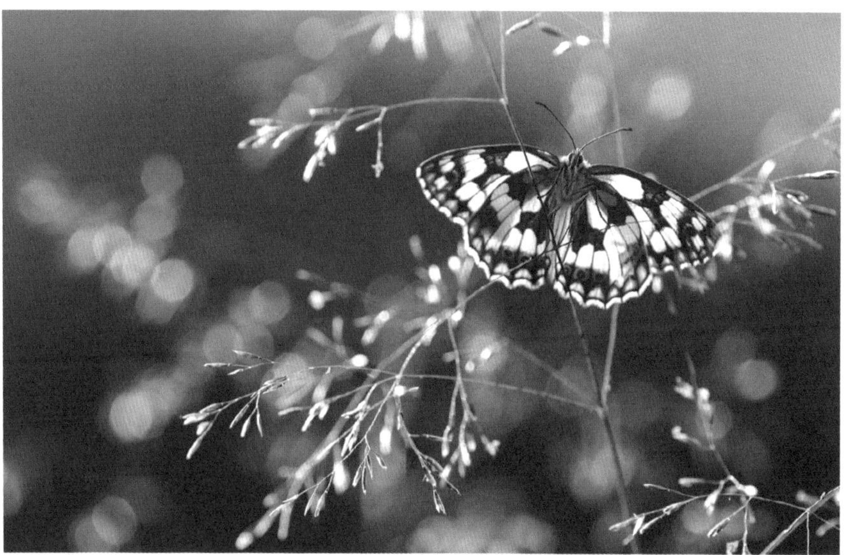

PRO TIPS

- To help you "see" in black and white, change your camera's picture style to Monochrome so the image preview (and Live View) appears without the distraction of color. Shoot in RAW format so the file still contains all the color information.

- Users of mirrorless cameras will benefit from seeing the subject in black and white through the camera's electronic viewfinder (EVF).

- Find inspiration by looking at the work of renowned fine-art photographers such as David Lloyd and David Yarrow, who both specialize in black-and-white nature photography.

- Adobe Lightroom, Photoshop, and Nik Silver Efex Pro are among the best editing programs for mono conversion.

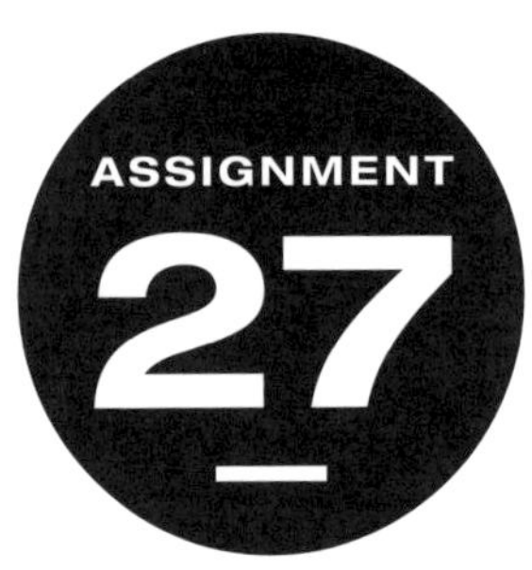

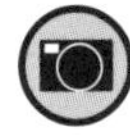
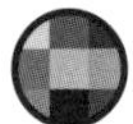
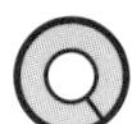

TECHNIQUE

- Shooting from low angles can prove awkward—a flip-out articulated LCD screen with Live View, or a right-angle viewfinder attachment, can help framing and focusing.

- Use a tripod with low-level capability or a beanbag.

FUN WITH FUNGI

For this assignment we're asking you to explore the hidden world at your feet, and shoot some images of fungi. Fungi often grow in dark, damp, and inaccessible places, but they look fascinating in frame-filling close-ups. They are at their peak in the fall, so be prepared to wait until then before you can fulfill this project.

To find subjects in prime, pristine condition, suited to creative photography, make regular visits to ancient woodland and carefully check decaying stumps, fallen branches, and leaf deposits. Be prepared to get down low and shoot from ground level to achieve the best perspective. A worm's-eye view (see page 26) often works well, particularly when photographing species with attractive gills. Backlighting— from sunlight, a small LED light, or a flashlight—can help highlight the shape, delicacy, and translucency of mushrooms. A macro lens or close-up attachment will normally be needed, but a wideangle lens can help create striking environmental studies.

As with all close-up subjects, limited depth of field is a common problem. Some types of fungi are awkwardly shaped—for instance, a toadstool's cap will extend closer to the camera's sensor plane than its stalk, making it hard to keep everything in focus. The exact aperture or f-stop will depend on the shape of your subject, the level of magnification, and the effect you desire, but you may need a small aperture to keep everything in focus. Experiment, but an aperture of f/8 is a good starting point. Now try shooting your own. Take a series of eight beautiful fungi shots and print them.

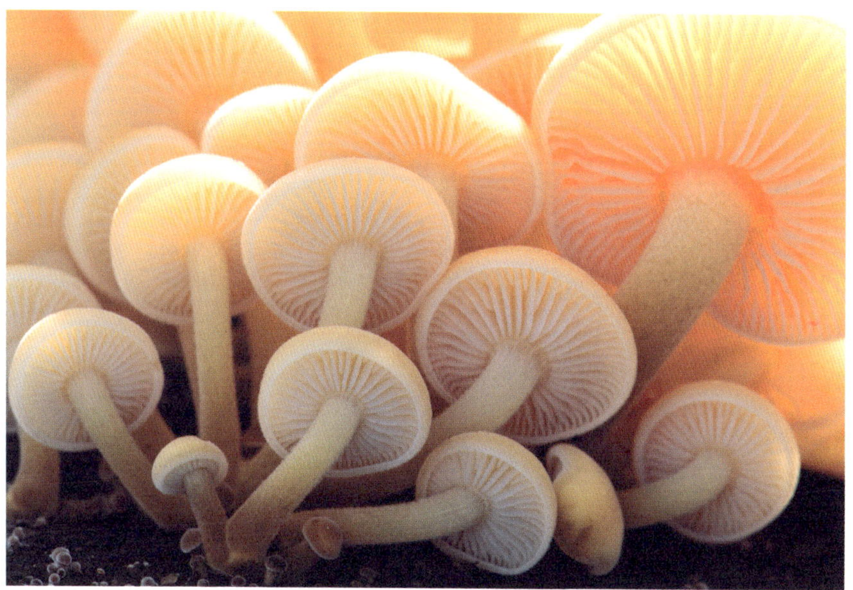

FIELD NOTES

- Light is often in short supply in dense woodland, so shutter speeds will be slow. Use a tripod and carry a small LED light for supplementary or creative lighting (see page 52). A reflector (see page 48) may also prove handy.

- Carry a groundsheet to help you keep yourself and your kit clean and dry.

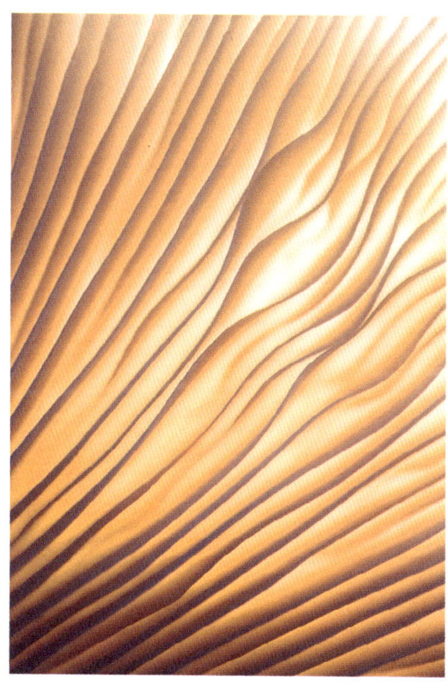

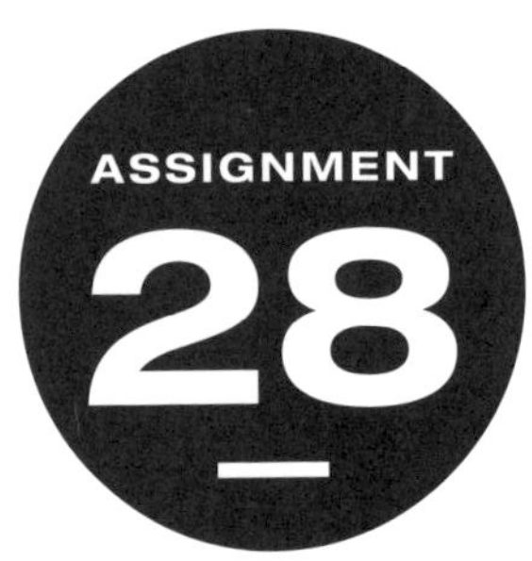

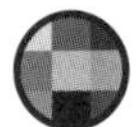
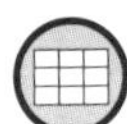

TECHNIQUE

- Light levels during the blue hour will typically be low, so keep an eye on your shutter speed and raise your ISO if you need to.

- The blue hour doesn't peak for long, so plan your shoots beforehand and visualize your images. Get into position well in advance and work out your exposures, so that when the optimum time comes you are ready to shoot and capture the moment.

- Silhouettes work particularly well at twilight (see page 40). Look for interesting cloud formations that you may be able to use as part of your compositions.

INTO THE BLUE

During the brief period before sunrise and following sunset, light temperature cools down and blue hues become more dominant. This is known as the "blue hour." Pictures taken at this time can possess a serene and ethereal quality, the blue tones evoking a dreamlike, magical mood. We would like you to make the most of this unique and transient light, and create five images that capture it at its best.

Be as creative as possible and avoid simply shooting the same images as you would normally. Think carefully about the way in which the light interacts with the subject. What type of animal, bird, or insect would suit an image with a tranquil mood? There will be much less light available at this time, making moving subjects difficult to capture, but why not take advantage of the low light levels and use the camera as a paintbrush (see page 116)? Long exposures are very effective in the blue hues of twilight.

You could juxtapose your subject against artificial lighting, and use the deep blues of the sky to create the atmosphere. Explore urban environments (see page 74) to see if it's possible to silhouette your subject against streetlamps, or in the tungsten light emanating from windows. Mid-sized zoom lenses—or even wideangle lenses—are more suited to this approach as you will need to compose a wider scene, creating a relationship between the subject, the light, and the environment.

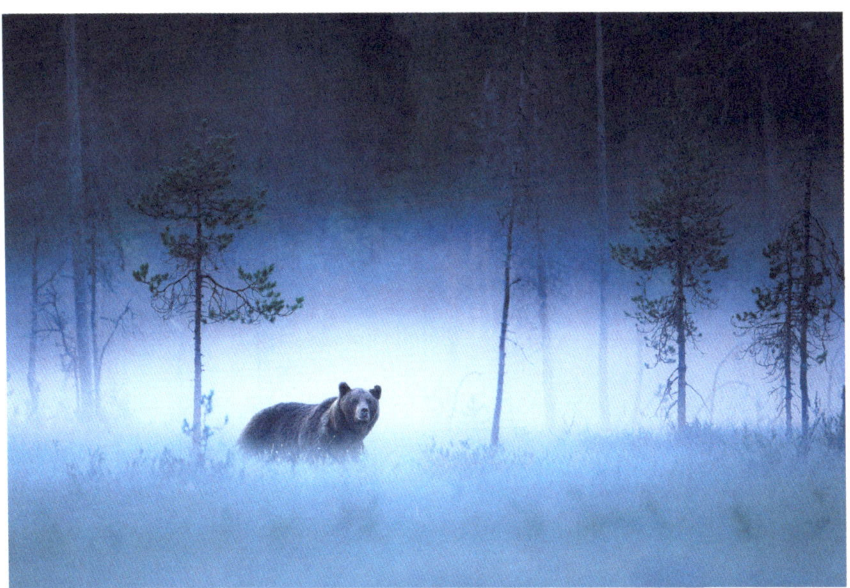

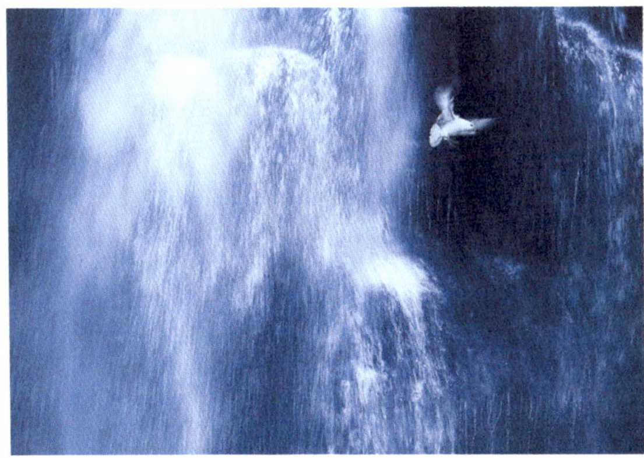

▲ *This brown bear was captured at 1 a.m. from a blind (or hide) in the Finnish taiga forest. It is so far north that there is no true darkness in summer, but the blue hour is spectacular and creates a special mood.*

◀ *This image of a fulmar in motion was taken a few minutes before sunrise, when deep, rich blues were evident in the light.*

FIELD NOTES

- Before you can exploit the blue hour to the full in your photography, it's a good idea to visit the location first. Stay out until after sunset and watch the sky. As the colors of the sun fade, they will be replaced by a deep, rich blue. Take plenty of test shots to work out your exposure. The light during the blue hour will be relatively flat, so expose to the right (see page 28) to maximize detail.

- Alternatively, you may find potential subjects in your garden—search for roosting insects, such as dragonflies and damselflies, and see if there is a way to silhouette them against the sky, or even the moon.

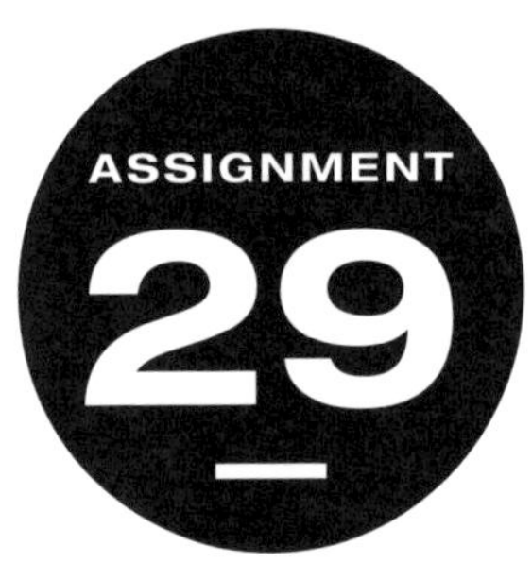

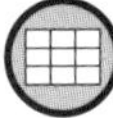

TECHNIQUE

- Camera setup will vary depending on the model, but typically the multiple exposure mode is found in the Shooting Menu. Switch it on and select the number of images you desire.

- Begin with just two, but if you want to be more daring and experimental, select a higher number of frames (most cameras offer a maximum of ten frames).

- Turn on Auto Gain so your camera automatically adjusts exposure gain for each additional image in order to create a correctly exposed final image.

DOUBLE VISION

For this project, we'd like you to be innovative. Most mirrorless and digital SLR cameras have a multiple exposure mode that allows you to capture and overlay two or more frames in-camera. You can use this function to create ethereal results by layering images together that are either framed or focused differently. You can instantly produce impressionistic results without resorting to Photoshop.

Once your camera is set up and multiple exposure activated, think carefully about subject choice. This technique suits wildflowers, foliage, and trees particularly well, but potentially anything can work. It's best to use a tripod, but you might prefer to work freehand, depending on the effect you wish to achieve. You really can have a lot of fun experimenting.

Although the technique is simple enough, shooting multiple exposures can be unpredictable. Be prepared to take lots of frames to get the result you desire. The creative potential is limitless, though. In addition to defocusing the lens, try creating a different interpretation of your subject by altering the composition or focal length for subsequent frames. Or even combining different approaches. To complete the brief, create three images of whatever subjects appeal to you, each using a different approach to multiple-exposure photography.

ORTON EFFECT

The most popular approach to multiple-exposure photography is to layer a sharp, in-focus frame with a subsequent one that is defocused and blurred. This simulates what is known as the Orton Effect—a creative technique that gives images a bright, dreamlike glow. Although it is easier to mimic the effect in post-processing software, such as Photoshop, it is far more satisfying and enjoyable to do it in-camera. Also, your images will then be eligible for being entered in many photography competitions (see page 124). Generally speaking, photo composites are not eligible for major contests.

PRO TIPS

• In addition to creating your multiple exposure image, most cameras will allow you to keep each frame in the sequence—useful should you later decide you don't like the effect.

▼ *The Orton Effect works particularly well with flowers, foliage, and backlit subjects.*

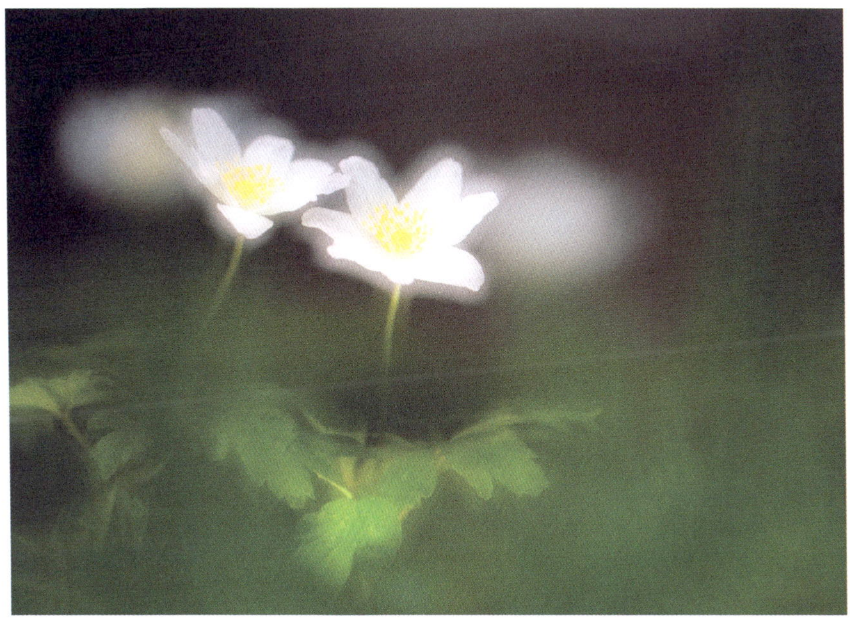

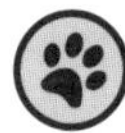

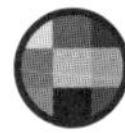

TECHNIQUE

- Nocturnal animals, such as foxes, are often still active at dawn. Heading out early may give you the opportunity to capture them in natural light before the streets start to get busy with people.

- Foxes are scavengers, so, where there is rubbish, there is a good chance a fox won't be too far away.

- Don't ignore smaller subjects. City gardens can attract all sorts of insects from bees to butterflies. Think of ways in which you can incorporate the urban environment into your compositions.

CITY SLICKERS

The increasing pressures on natural habitats and the abundance of food and nesting sites in urban areas mean that towns and cities are fast becoming havens for wildlife.

For this assignment, we would like you to capture an image that shows your subject in the urban environment in which it lives. You will need to think carefully about not only the subject but ways in which you can incorporate the urban landscape. City parks are great places to explore. The wildlife will probably be accustomed to people. Why not use this to your advantage and choose a wideangle lens to show the subject and the surroundings in the same image?

A lens with a short focal length will give an entirely different perspective to that of a long telephoto lens, and it can be used to exaggerate perspective and give an increased perception of depth. Don't be afraid of including people in your compositions. Showing the way in which people and wildlife are connected would be an interesting theme to explore.

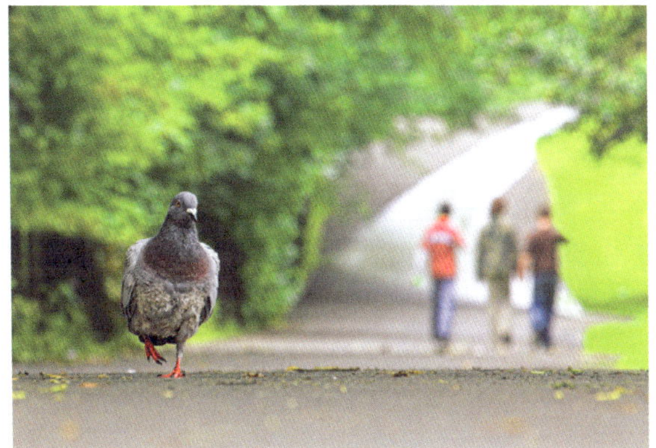

▲ *A medium telephoto zoom was used here to focus on the bird while the large aperture threw the background out of focus. The people are an important part of the image, and tell the story of urban wildlife.*

▼ *With the abundance of prey and suitability of large buildings for nesting sites, many cities throughout the world are now home to nesting peregrine falcons. Photographing rare birds at their nest—especially birds of prey—often requires a licence, so check the law where you live (see page 111).*

FIELD NOTES

- There is no escaping the fact that working with long lenses may attract unwanted attention. Always be aware of your surroundings and stay vigilant and safe. If you can, keep to crowded areas and avoid any situations with which you are not completely comfortable.

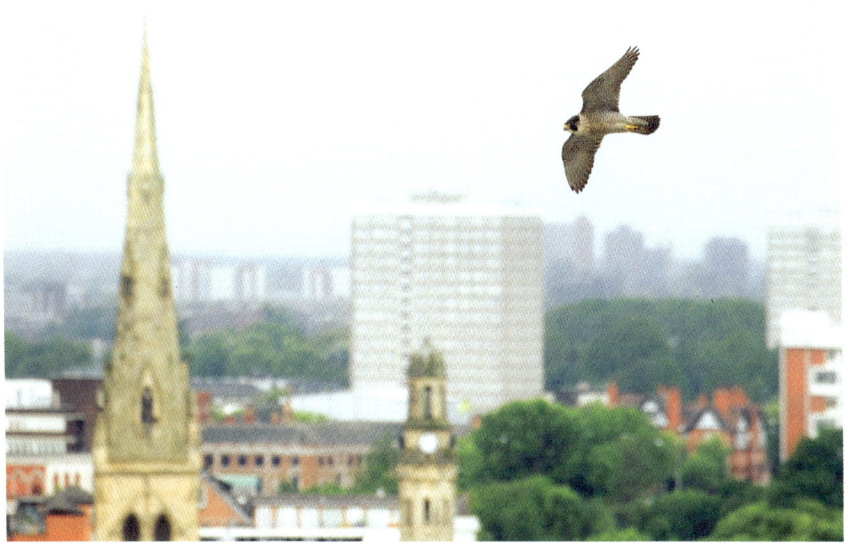

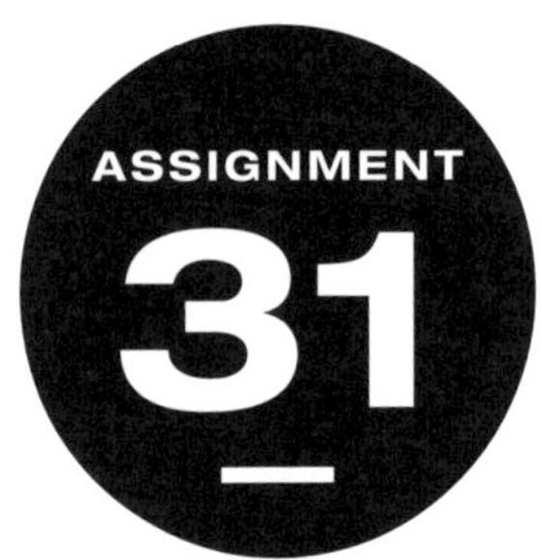

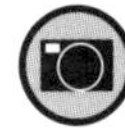
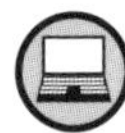
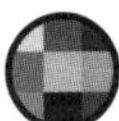

TECHNIQUE

- You don't have to rely on your camera's white balance (WB) presets for this assignment. Most cameras allow you to dial in your own custom Kelvin (K) value. This typically has a range of 2500–10,000K; the higher the value, the warmer the color temperature.

- Dialing in a warm WB setting, like Shade, is an effective way to enhance colorful sunsets.

NATURAL BALANCE

Don't underestimate how much color temperature can influence the look and feel of your nature photography (see page 42). Warmer tones are uplifting, while bluer hues convey a feeling of coolness or nighttime. Cameras have a white balance (WB) setting to allow you to alter the color temperature of images. This is primarily for neutralizing color casts produced by various light sources to create natural-looking photographs, and there are presets to mimic common types of light, including Daylight, Cloudy, Shade, and Incandescent. Cameras also have an Auto WB setting, which accurately records the light's temperature. However, these tools make it possible to change the hue of an image for creative purposes, which is what we want you to do here.

Take a series of shots of the same subject using each one of your camera's WB presets. Shade will warm up your shot, while Incandescent cools things down, for instance. Compare your images side by side. Now apply what you've learned creatively. Try to deliberately mismatch WB to create obvious and dramatic color casts to your shots. This will add visual impact. Select your subject carefully—scenes containing white, light tones often work well, particularly backlit subjects or animals in silhouette (see pages 24 and 40). Select three different shots that use WB creatively and print them out to complete the assignment. You can also adjust the color temperature of RAW files at the post-processing stage. Therefore, this assignment can be completed in the field or on your computer.

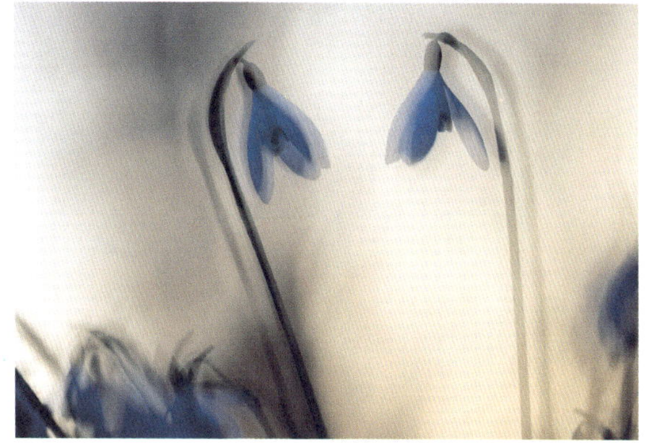

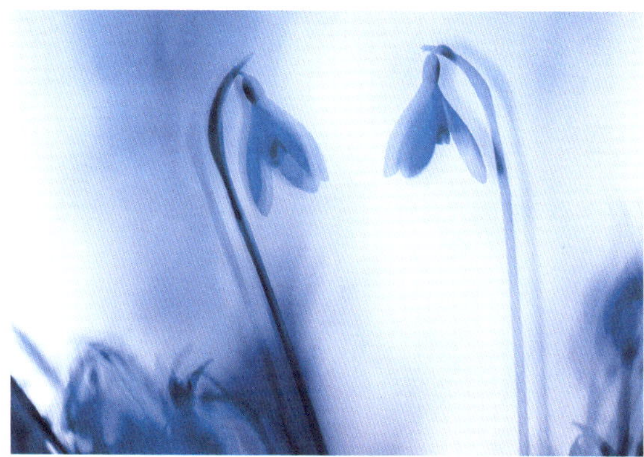

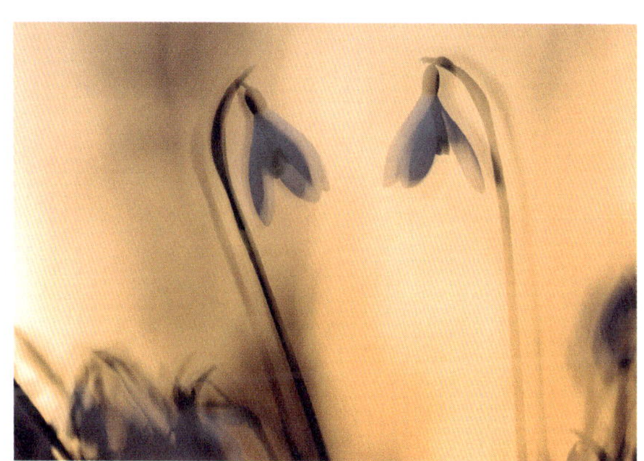

◀ *This snowdrop image is shown with different WB settings, from the top: Auto, Incandescent, and Shade. If you shoot in RAW format, you can quickly and precisely adjust WB when editing your shots—even the most basic RAW converter allows you to do this. However, if you capture JPEGs, it is important to record WB the way you want it in-camera when you release the shutter.*

FIELD NOTES

- To help exaggerate the coolness of wintry conditions, such as ice and snow, deliberately select a cooler color temperature to add a subtle blue tone to your shots and emphasize the freezing conditions.

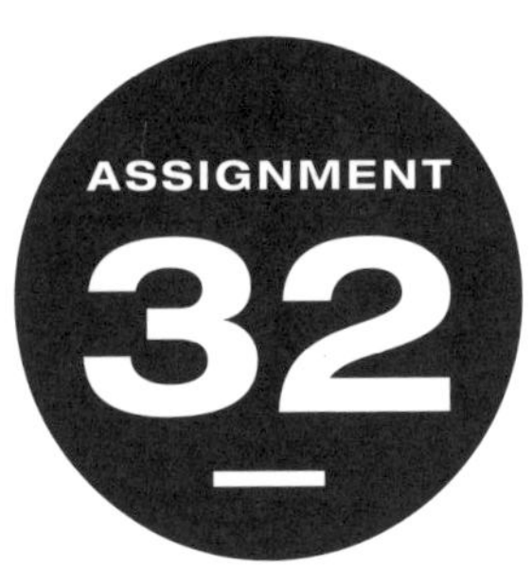

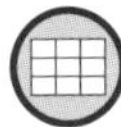

TECHNIQUE

- Individual images are rarely as effective as a series of shots taken over days, weeks, or even years that collectively tell a story and communicate changes to a habitat or individual species.

- Try teaming up with local wildlife organizations or conservation groups. Your images can be used to help them convey their message.

- Images that capture interaction between people and nature are always powerful and useful—for example, children pond dipping, habitat restoration, tree planting, or a beach clean. It is not always the "pretty" nature shots that are the most effective at telling the story.

STORY TIME

Why do you enjoy nature photography? Most wildlife photographers have a deep-rooted passion for the natural world, and seeing and experiencing nature is their main motivation—the camera is simply a tool to record, share, or interpret those experiences. But photographs can be so much more—they can tell a story and speak far louder than any words. They play an essential role in conservation efforts around the world, communicating the plight of endangered species and habitat loss. Could your photographs help conservation efforts?

This assignment is different to all the others. We want you to use your nature photography to benefit your subjects and the ecosystems we share. What stories can you tell? Start by looking locally. For instance, is there a development that threatens a local wood, meadow, or wetland? Use your images to communicate that habitat's importance to wildlife, as well as its benefits for people. If there is an action group, contact them and offer your skills as a visual artist. You may have existing images you can donate, or you may need to capture specific shots.

Visual imagery can encourage empathy and you can use that to raise awareness and inspire action to help your local wildlife and community. Nature photographers have an important role to play in conservation, and we hope you'll continue to employ your skills to help wildlife beyond this single assignment.

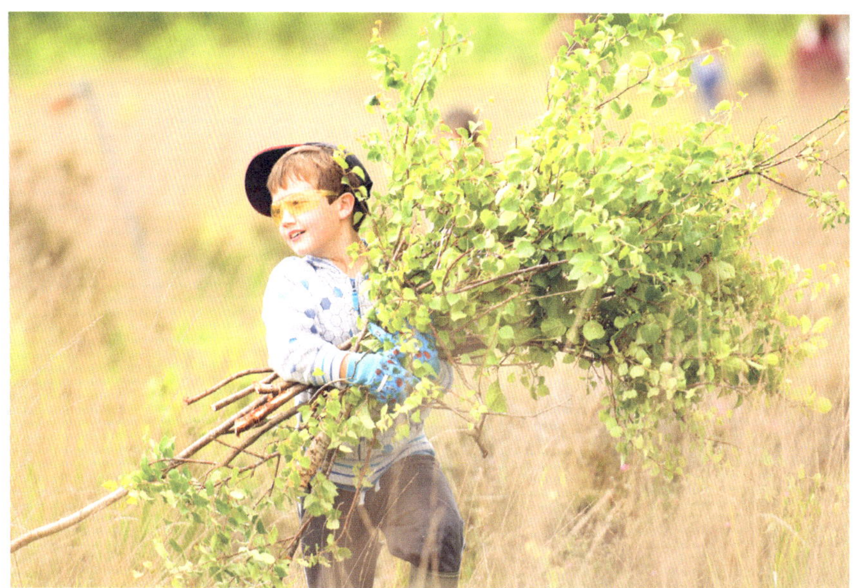

▲ *Visual communication is essential for championing conservation, habitat restoration, and rewilding.*

▼ *Photographs showing interaction between animals and people help to promote the importance of healthy relationships with the natural world.*

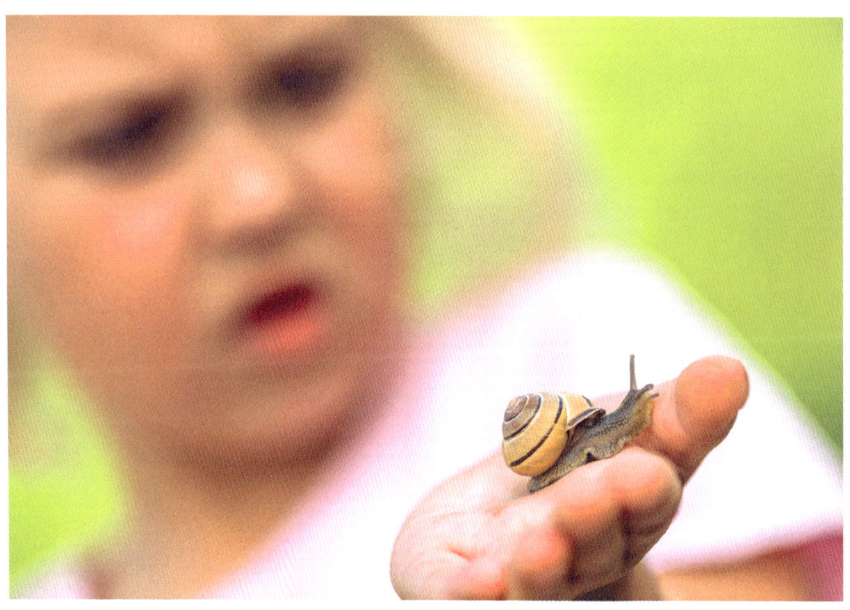

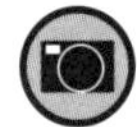

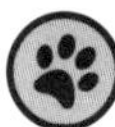
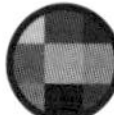

TECHNIQUE

- Compared to wild deer, park deer are usually more tolerant of humans, but they can still be difficult to approach. Move slowly, and stop every now and again to let them grow accustomed to your presence.

- When covering large distances, it is important to travel light—take just one camera body and one lens. A telephoto zoom lens (such as a 100–400mm lens) will provide you with the flexibility you need in composing your shots, while also being light and easy to handle.

- A monopod will provide support for your lens, but will also be lighter to carry than a tripod and quicker to set up.

PARK LIFE

Deer make fantastic subjects for wildlife photographs. Not only are they impressive-looking animals, but the many parks where they live are accessible, too. For this assignment, we would like you to visit a deer park and capture five images that give an insight into the lives of these majestic mammals.

We recommend visiting your chosen park several times to become familiar with the location and the deer, and the way they move around. Pay attention to the position and quality of the light. By far the best time of year to capture action is in the fall, during the rutting period. At this time of year stags will be roaring threats and battling for supremacy. To photograph action successfully, you will need to use a fast shutter speed, so, depending on the light, you may need to raise your ISO setting.

Time your visits to make the most of morning and evening light, and look for different weather conditions. Shooting bursts of images using your camera's high-speed drive mode will help you to capture the best of the action. Think carefully about backgrounds, too—moving just a few feet to one side can dramatically change an image.

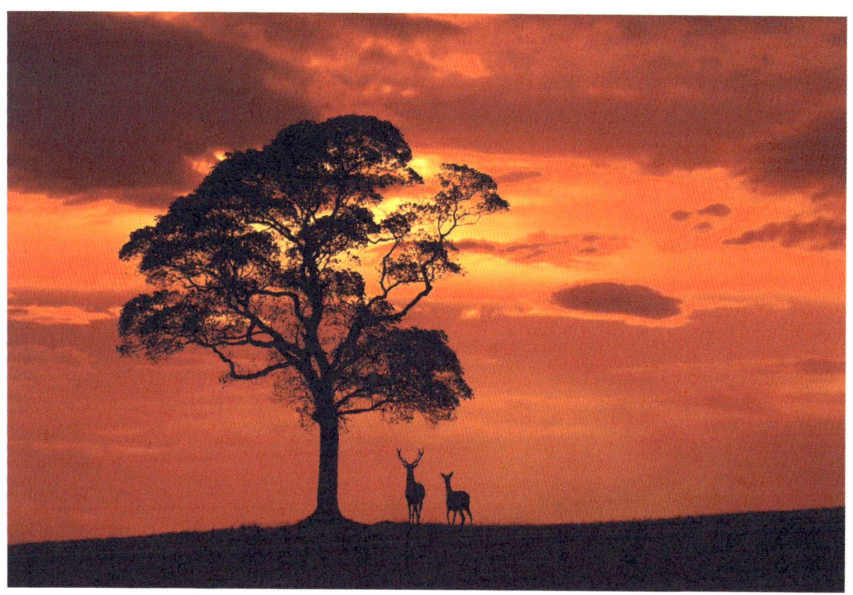

▲ Deer have a distinctive shape which works well as a silhouette, and parks with large areas of open ground offer horizons you can use to capture images of deer against the sky.

▼ No matter how many times you visit the same location to capture the same subjects, there will always be something new that adds variety to your images, such as weather conditions.

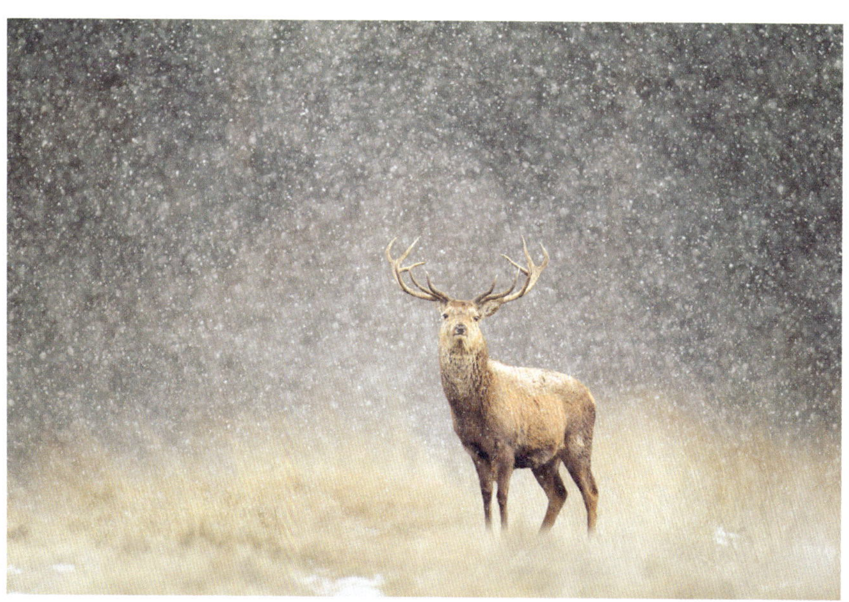

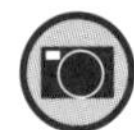

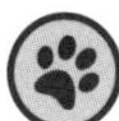
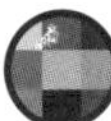

TECHNIQUE

- Due to the dense tree canopy overhead, light is often limited within a woodland–select a higher ISO of 1600–3200 to generate a fast enough shutter speed.

- Opt for a wideangle lens to show your subject in its woodland setting.

- Use a macro lens for mosses, lichens, liverworts, and fungi (see page 68).

FIELD NOTES

- Visit woodland throughout the year to build a diverse portfolio of images.

- Golden, dappled sunlight pouring through the trees at dawn and dusk can produce magical conditions for nature photography.

WOODLAND WILDLIFE

If you go down to the woods today, you're sure of a big surprise… Forests are a rich habitat for a huge range of plants and animals. Your brief is to take a series of photographs within a woodland, under the leaf canopy. The more time you can dedicate to this project, the better your images will be. Shortlist a set of five images that collectively show the woodland's extraordinary biodiversity.

Of all woodland wildlife, birds are the most obvious group, but they can prove tricky to get close to. See if you can get access to private woodland and ask permission from the landowner to set up a blind or hide (see page 56) and feeders (see page 14). Birds will quickly take advantage of any food you put out.

Deer and squirrels that roam among the trees and in public parks will already be quite accustomed to humans, making them easier to approach and photograph. In spring, ancient deciduous woodland floors will be covered in wildflowers, offering a great spectacle and a chance for beautiful images.

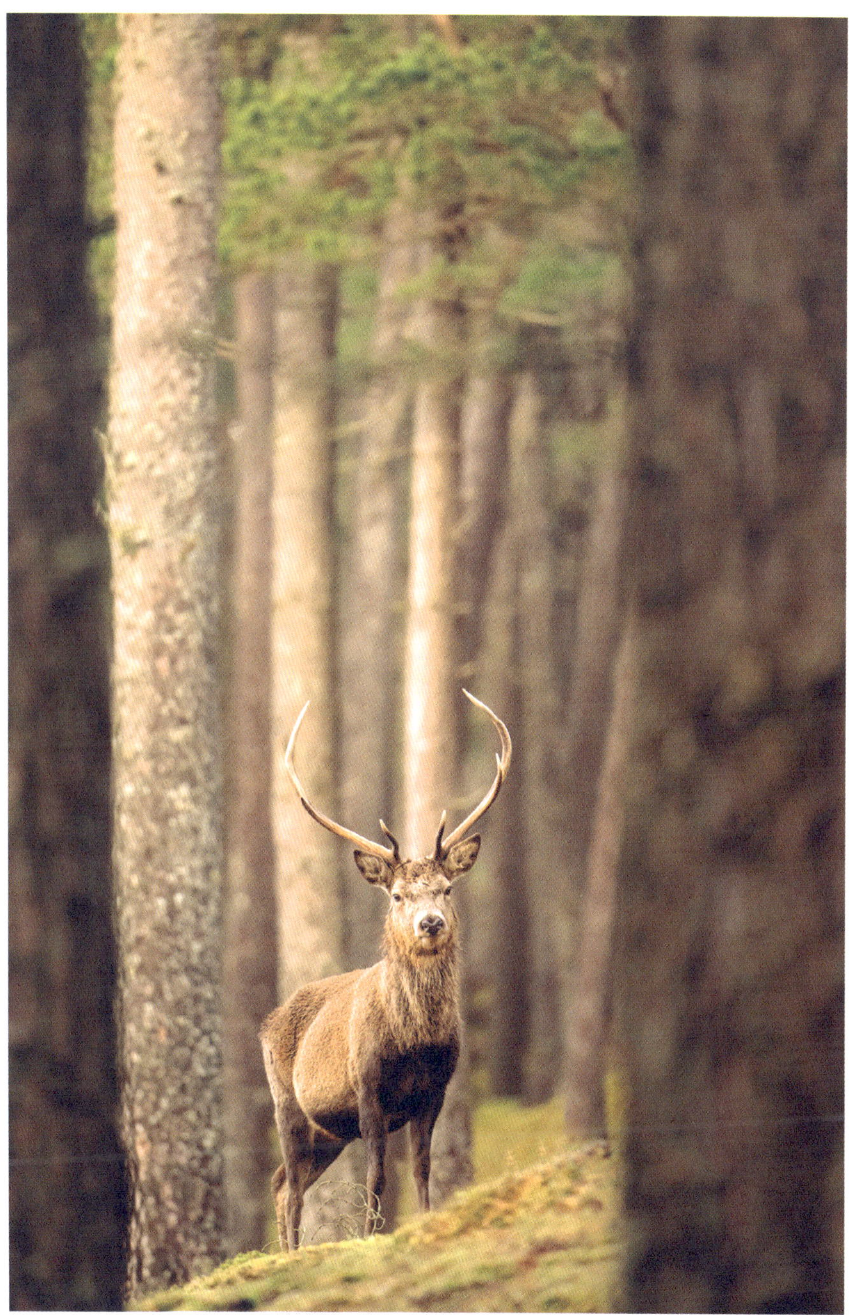

▲ *Tree trunks and branches can provide a framing aid for mammals and birds. Use a long lens and large aperture to direct the viewer's eye between them to your subject.*

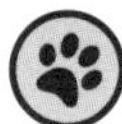 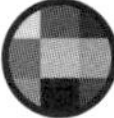

TECHNIQUE

- Small seabirds, such as puffins, are fast flyers. Use a shutter speed of at least 1/2000 sec. to freeze their movement.

- On a clear day in summer, the light will be harsh for most of the time. Pay careful attention to your exposures and try to avoid losing highlight detail by dialing in negative exposure compensation as needed.

FIELD NOTES

- Shoot subjects on the ground from a low angle. If your tripod has a center column that can't be removed or repositioned at 90°, use a beanbag.

- Shoot some images with a wideangle lens—this will help to capture the birds in their dramatic surroundings.

ISLAND LIFE

For those who don't have enough time to dedicate weeks or months to specific projects, visiting a seabird colony over a day or a weekend may be the answer, offering plenty of photographic opportunities in just a few hours. To complete this assignment, head off to an island nature reserve in the spring or summer and create a portfolio of at least eight images from your visit.

During the breeding season, you are likely to be faced with an overwhelming number of birds. This can be confusing at first, but spend some time observing and you should soon learn to find where to set up. Rather than take an image of one bird and move on to another, stick with just one or two subjects for as long as you can. This should ensure you can capture behavior and create images that tell a story.

For portraits, keep things simple. Look for birds in an open area, free from clutter. A large aperture will reduce depth of field and separate the subject from its surroundings. Get down as low as you can to include a diffused foreground— this adds depth and leads the viewer's eye to the subject.

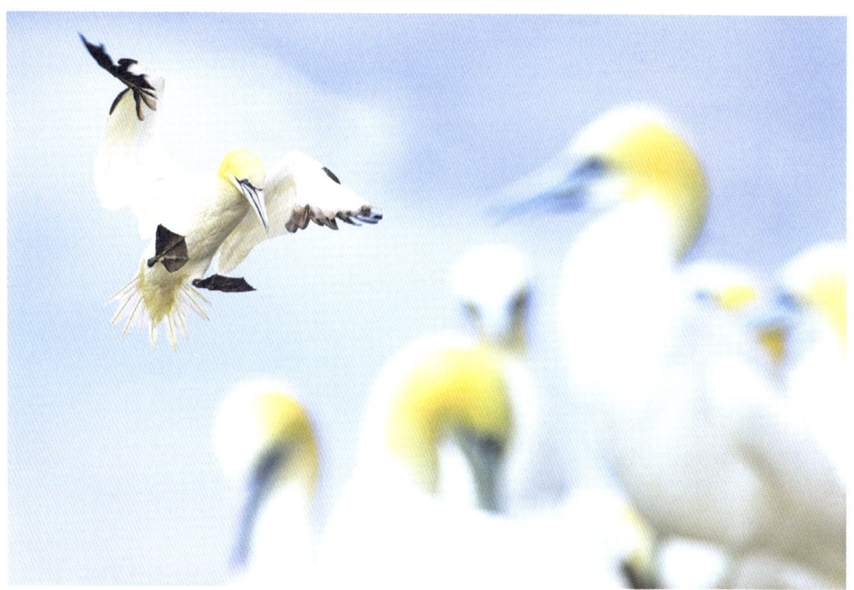

▲ *Including a group of out-of-focus birds in the foreground has increased depth and added interest to this composition.*

▼ *This puffin was photographed at ground level, using a beanbag for camera support. The diffused foreground adds depth and leads the viewer's eye straight to the bird.*

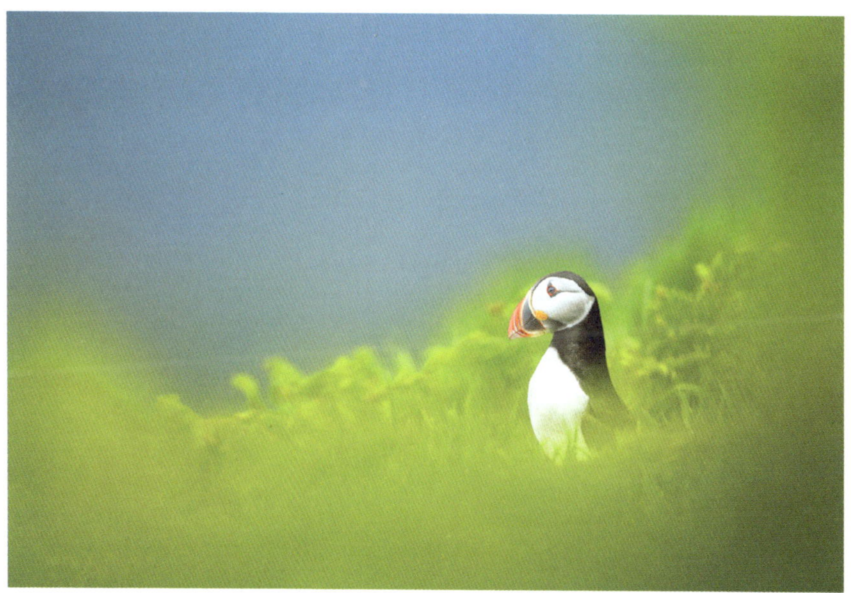

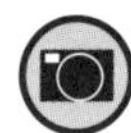

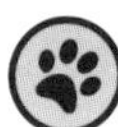
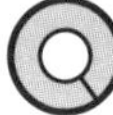

TECHNIQUE

- Hone your close-up photography skills by visiting a butterfly house. Captive butterflies will sit still for long periods, allowing you to practice your approach and technique.

- Ensure your subject stands out against the background by selecting an aperture small enough to keep your subject sharp throughout, but large enough to throw background detail out of focus—f/8 is a good starting point.

FIELD NOTES

- Visit a flower meadow just after sunrise, wait for it to warm up and butterflies to awaken and bask in the morning sunshine—this will enable you to photograph them before they become too active and flighty.

BUTTERFLY EFFECT

In spring and summer, you can find colorful, beautiful butterflies almost anywhere, from meadows, verges, and woodland glades to your own garden. For this assignment, seek out these delicate insects, and take four photographs, each with a different creative approach. But you will need to be patient. Butterflies are flighty and can be very hard to approach closely enough to photograph.

Research good butterfly habitats close to where you live. Anywhere that has lots of flowers should be home to a good range of species in the spring and summer. Butterflies are easiest to find during the height of the day, when they will be busily feeding on nectar-rich plants. Stalk the butterflies carefully, using a macro lens, or a telephoto lens coupled with a close-up filter (see page 20) or extension tube. Watch where your shadow falls—if it covers your subject, it will almost certainly fly away. Tread carefully, too—disturbing nearby grasses, flowers, or foliage will scare the butterfly. If the insect does take flight, wait for it to settle and start your approach again.

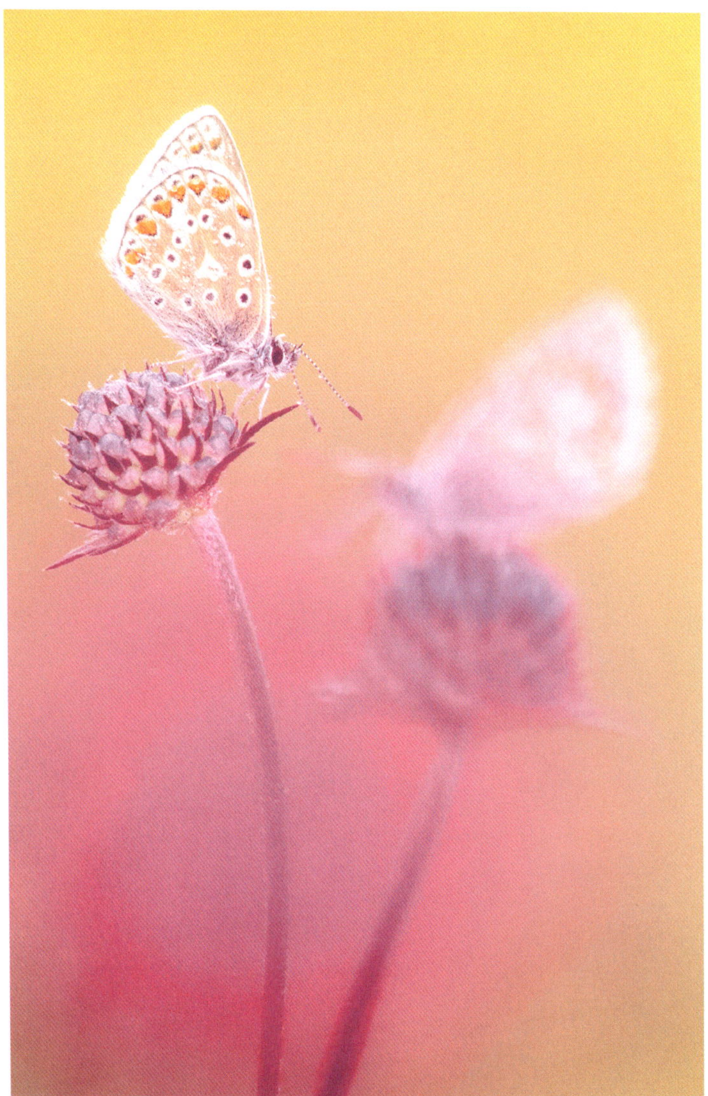

PRO TIPS

• Don't always shoot a top-down view of a butterfly with its wings open—try a head-on portrait, or shoot its underwings from the side.

• You don't always need to fill the frame with your subject. Some negative space (see page 12) will add context and scale.

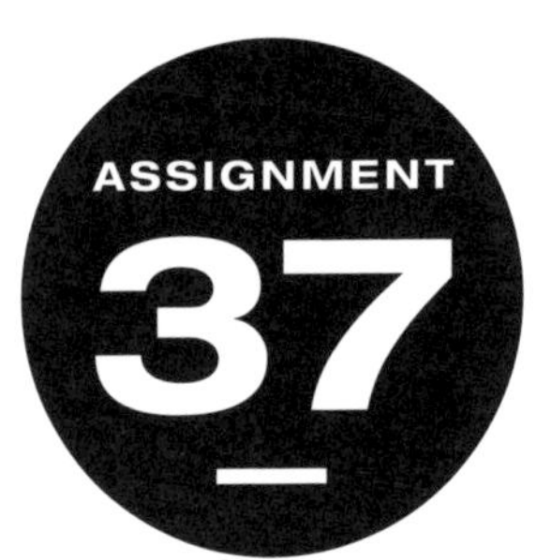

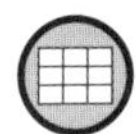

TECHNIQUE

- If you are shooting in urban areas, show a sense of the place in the image by using a wideangle lens.

- Visit your chosen location at different times of the day. Dawn and dusk are usually most productive as wildlife tends to be more active at these times.

- Be innovative—look at your images and think of ways in which you can vary your compositions and show your subjects in a different light.

MAP CHALLENGE

Nature photography demands knowledge not only of your subject, but also of a location. It is no coincidence that, in most cases, a photographer's most successful images are those taken close to where they live. For this project, we would like you to open Google Maps, set a radius of 10 miles (16km) from your home, and create a portfolio of eight images taken only within this area.

Whether you live in the country or in the middle of a city, there are plenty of potential subjects if you look closely enough. For those that live in or near the countryside, look for areas of woodland to explore (see page 82), or perhaps you have a local nature reserve close by with purpose-built blinds (or hides). Ponds and lakes can be magnets for all kinds of creatures, from dragonflies and damselflies to various species of wildfowl. Wildlife is becoming more commonplace in urban areas (see page 74), and quiet areas in suburbia, such as cemeteries, can also offer refuge to all sorts of birds and animals.

Try to be creative in your approach and look for different species to photograph. Take the time to make lots of visits, and try different times of the year. As the seasons change, so too will the wildlife. Have fun exploring near to home.

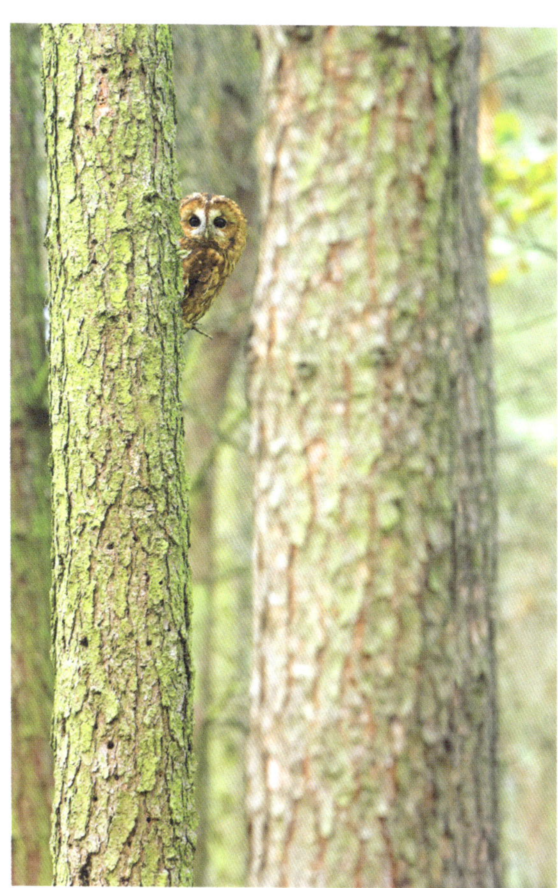

◄ *This tawny owl was photographed while exploring some local woodland. It was a completely unexpected but wonderful encounter.*

▼ *Several return visits had to be made to this local pond—where a cormorant had taken up residence for a week—before it was possible to capture the bird with prey.*

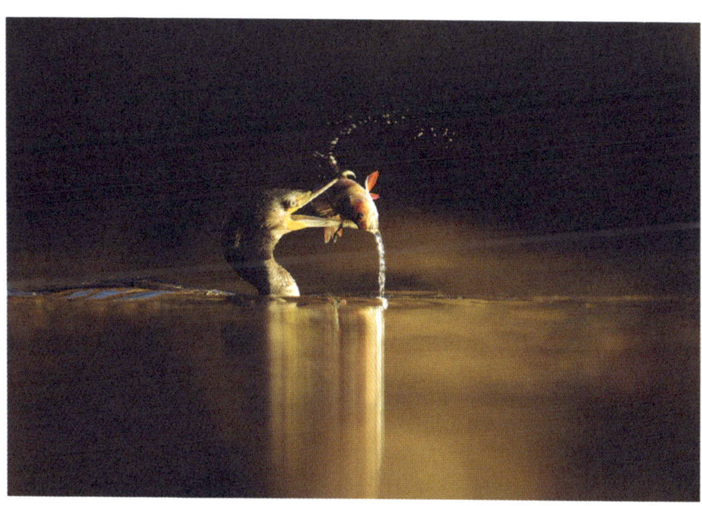

ASSIGNMENT 38

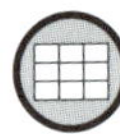

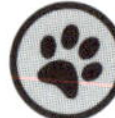

TECHNIQUE

- An exchange between a mother and its young can last for the briefest instant. By keeping your camera set to high-speed drive mode and firing a burst of images, you will give yourself the best chance of capturing the perfect moment.

- A tight crop will keep emphasis on the subject, but other subjects may suit a wider frame, capturing the surrounding habitat, so use a telephoto zoom lens to give yourself flexibility in composition.

▼ *Firing a burst of images made it easier to capture the moment these Galapagos sea lions touched noses.*

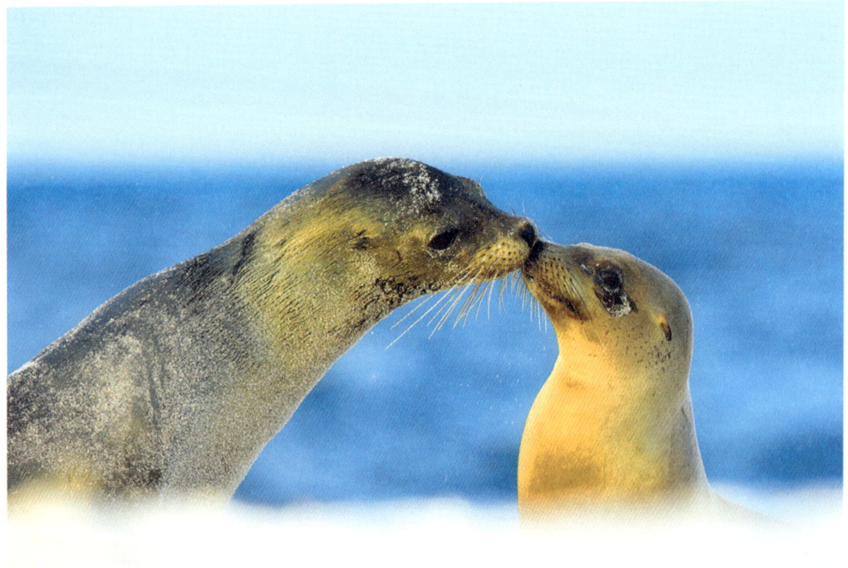

MOTHER AND CHILD

A truly successful nature photograph should create an immediate connection with the viewer. One way to achieve this is to elicit an emotional response, for instance by depicting a tender moment between a mother and its young. Your objective is to capture an image that creates this connection. As always, keep things simple. Try to visualize your image and stick rigidly to your end goal.

Your best chance for photographing these moments is in late spring and summer, when there is an abundance of new arrivals in the animal kingdom. Your local park will be home to families of ducks or perhaps swans with newborn cygnets. Between May and July, red deer give birth to their calves, and sea cliffs will be full of nesting seabirds. There is no shortage of potential subjects.

Pick one or two locations and visit them regularly to observe the birds and animals that can be found there. You should soon start to get an idea of the type of image you will be able to capture, and you will naturally find yourself visualizing pictures.

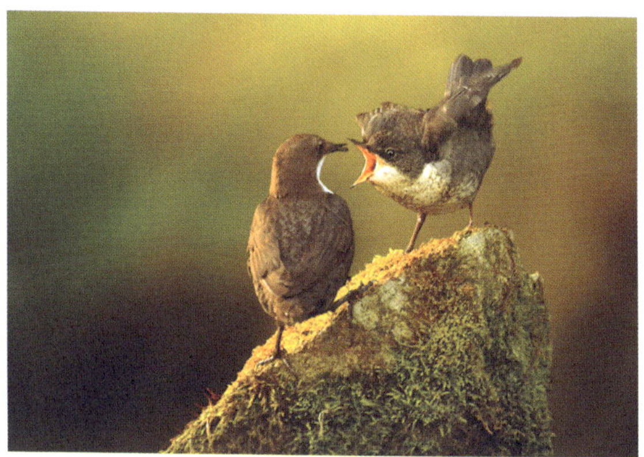

◀ *This dipper was photographed feeding its young well away from its nest to avoid any possible disturbance. Certain birds and animals can be extra-sensitive during the breeding season.*

FIELD NOTES

- When deciding on which subject to tackle, keep your options open. While it is good practice to visualize your images, don't ignore other more spontaneous opportunities that come your way. Always keep a close eye on your surroundings, and be ready to react at a moment's notice.

- In the breeding season, birds and animals become more susceptible to disturbance. Be especially careful when approaching subjects with young, and never encroach to the point their behavior becomes unnatural. The welfare of your subjects must always come first (see page 111 for more on wildlife photography ethics and the law).

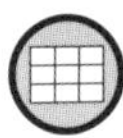
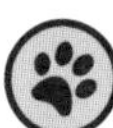

TECHNIQUE

- It takes time and practice to capture the decisive moment, so be patient. The right moment could be anything from a tender touch between a mother and her young to two stags fighting for supremacy.

FIELD NOTES

- Spend lots of time observing your subject. Record your observations in a notebook. You will start to notice patterns that will help you to be in the right place at the right time.

THE DECISIVE MOMENT

Capturing a moment that tells a story is a powerful way of raising an emotional response and creating a connection between subject and viewer. Achieving this requires patience and quick reactions: hesitate and the moment can be lost forever.

To begin your assignment, choose a subject where there is a good chance of interaction, such as a pair of displaying birds or a mother nurturing her young (see page 90). Spend as much time as possible observing and photographing your subject—this will provide a greater chance of capturing the decisive moment. Where there are lots of potential subjects, concentrate on just one or two pairs, and stay with them for as long as possible. Watch them closely and note patterns in their behavior, helping you to predict their next move.

The guidance on capturing the decisive moment continues on pages 94–5.
To complete your assignment, print two of your favorite images.

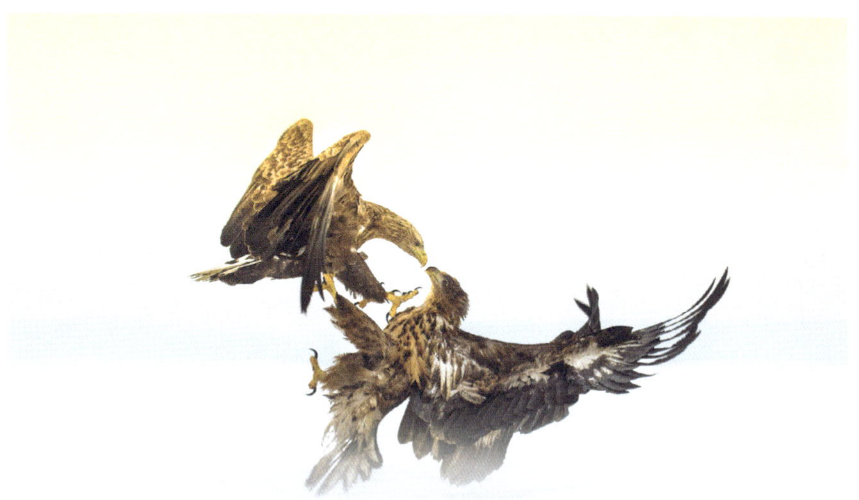

▲ *Images showing aggression, such as these sea eagles fighting over prey in the snow, can convey a sense of power and struggle.*

▼ *A wideangle lens was used to increase the field of view in this image, and give a greater chance of capturing the dolphins as they exited the water. Setting the camera to high-speed drive mode allows you to shoot in bursts, and then pick the best of the images.*

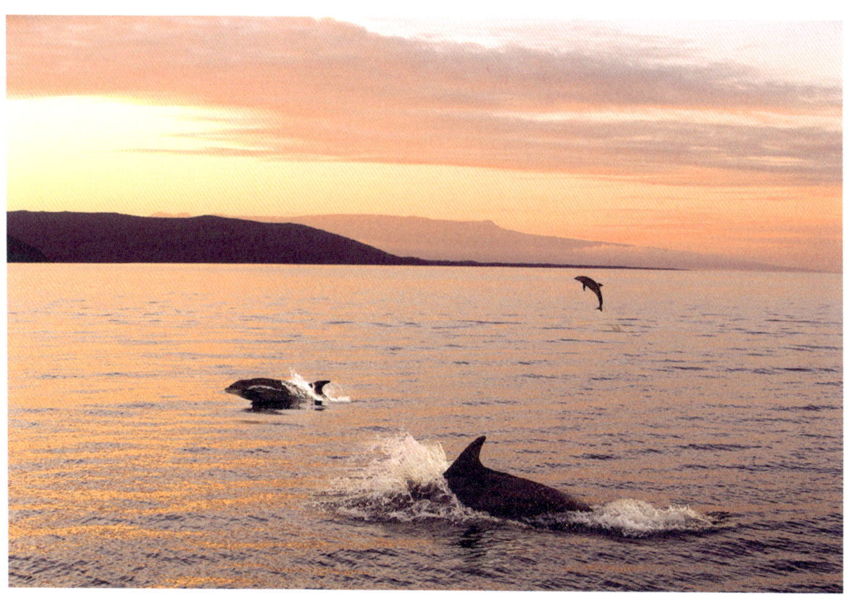

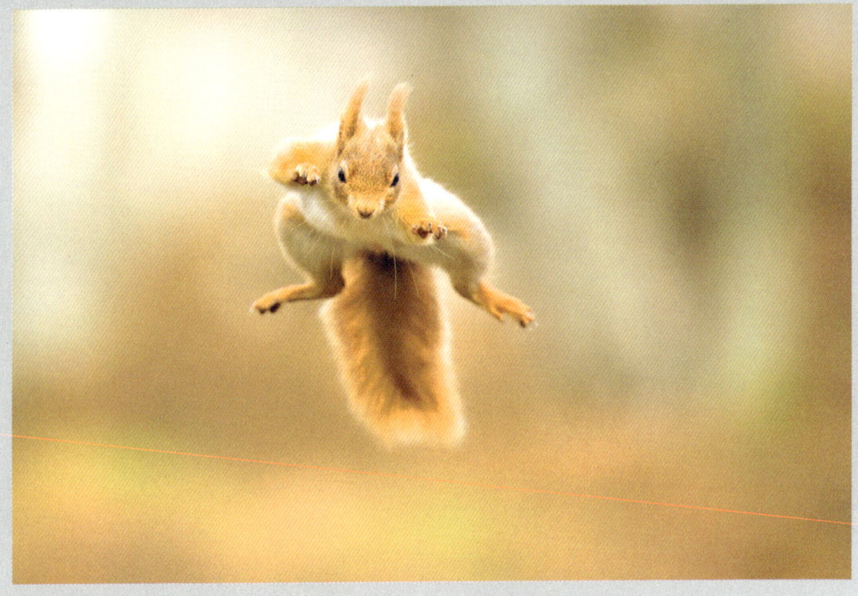

▲ *Capturing a burst of images in high-speed drive mode increased the chances of securing a successful picture of this red squirrel in mid-air.*

IMPROVE YOUR HIT RATE

Adopting a careful and deliberate approach will ensure you capture more decisive moments than you miss.

- For species that are largely inactive, you will need both patience and concentration. Mountain hares, for instance, will often crouch in heather and remain very still for long periods.

- The unexpected can occur at any given moment. A sudden stretch, a yawn, or simply a movement of the head can vastly improve an otherwise mundane portrait.

- Focus on your subject at all times, constantly recomposing your images in-camera with your finger ready to release the shutter.

- When framing your subject, don't ignore your surroundings. Study and analyze the whole frame, making sure to avoid any distractions or clutter in the image, and make any adjustments necessary to hone your composition. This way, as soon as the magic moment happens, you will be ready to capture it.

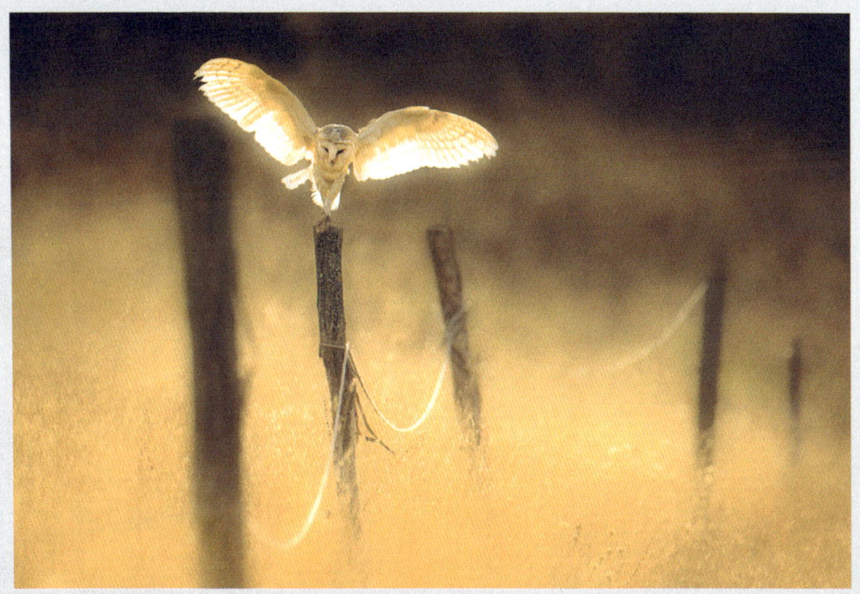

▲ *The decisive moment may only last for a split second, so make sure you always have your image composed and are ready to press the shutter release. The posts in this image act as a leading line, taking the viewer's eye through the frame.*

PRO TIPS

- Get to know your camera. Practice changing settings without taking your eye away from the viewfinder. This will make a huge difference when quick reactions are required.

- For a greater success rate, shoot on high-speed or "burst" drive mode, which enables you to shoot several images in a very short time.

- Avoid checking images on the LCD screen unless it is absolutely necessary—this will help you avoid missing a sudden movement.

- Don't forget to pay careful attention to the background. If there are any distracting elements, shift position to remove them from the frame.

ASSIGNMENT JOURNAL

____

____

____

____

____

____

____

____

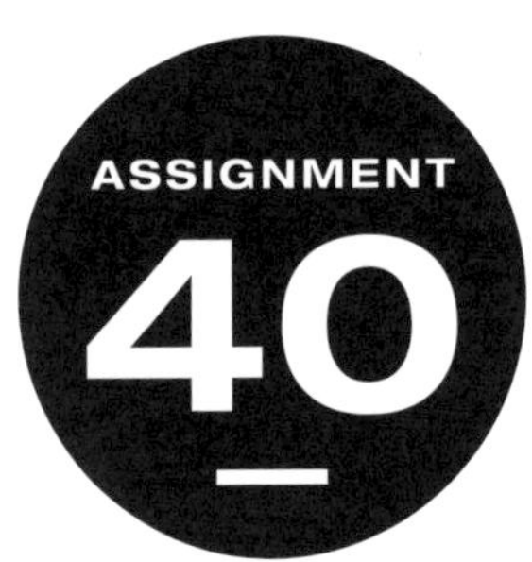

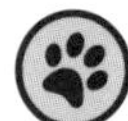
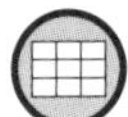

TECHNIQUE

- Visit a wildlife park early, or stay late, when there are fewer people getting in the way of photography.

- Observe one species and photograph it well, rather than rush about taking lots of images of different animals.

- Only visit a wildlife park, zoo, or rehabilitation center which is ethical and promotes conservation. The subject's welfare and wellbeing are always priorities.

CAPTIVE SUBJECT

Understandably, using captive subjects is a contentious issue. While the authors favor photographing animals in the wild, using fieldcraft and subject knowledge (see pages 60 and 64) to create images, photographing captive subjects is a wonderful way to hone your technique. It is also possible to take great animal photographs when your budget doesn't allow you to photograph a species in their country of origin.

For this assignment, your brief is to visit a wildlife park or center and take a set of natural-looking shots in a few hours. This is an ideal project if you are relatively inexperienced, or have limited free time, and want to refine your camera skills and learn to adjust camera settings more intuitively under less pressure, as well as learn how to anticipate and react to behavior. Your appreciation of nature will also grow as a result of getting close to normally timid or inaccessible species.

Think carefully about the background. If your subject is positioned close to a fence, wall, or railings, you will struggle to capture a flattering image. Bide your time and wait until the animal is within a more natural-looking setting. A simple change in shooting angle can be the answer. Use the longest lens practical. Telephotos foreshorten perspective and help to throw background detail out of focus, keeping images appearing natural.

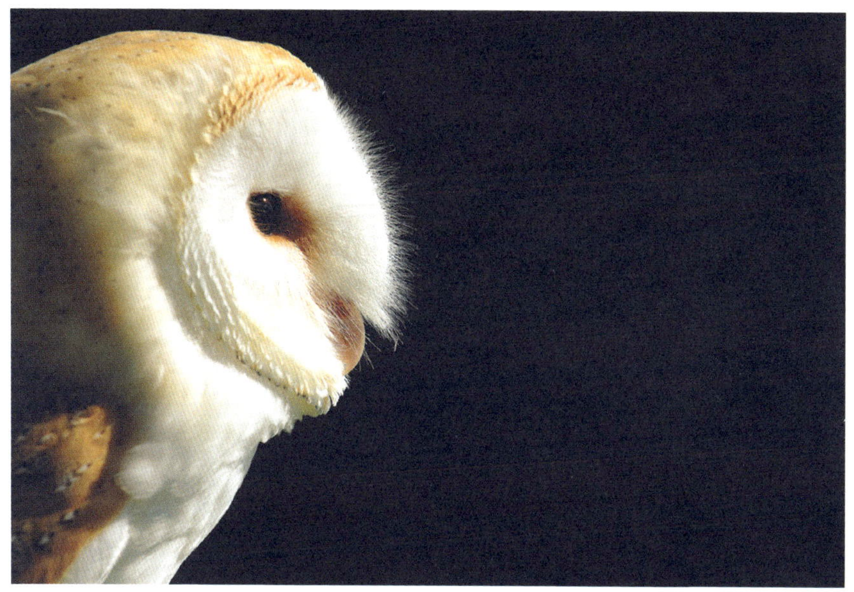

▲ *When it is otherwise impossible to hide or exclude the subject's enclosure, use a telephoto lens to isolate your subject and capture a frame-filling portrait.*

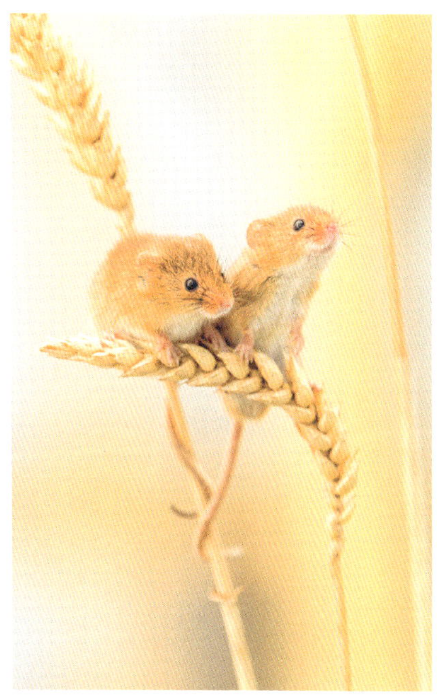

PRO TIPS

- Attach a lens hood. This will help to protect the front element when pushing your lens up close to fencing, and block out stray light when shooting through glass.

- When sharing images of captive wildlife, always declare that the animals were photographed in captivity. It is dishonest and disrespectful to the viewer and other nature photographers to try to pass off an image taken in a controlled environment as shot in the wild.

◀ *Be patient. Just because a subject is captive, it doesn't mean it is easy to capture a good shot. Be prepared to sit and wait to shoot the best pose, good eye contact, or interaction.*

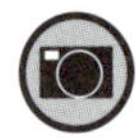

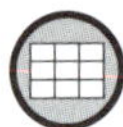
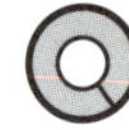

TECHNIQUE

- Wildflowers provide opportunities for all kinds of images, from frame-filling close-ups to wideangle views of carpets of color, so you can carry any type of lens to suit your vision. However, a dedicated macro lens is the best choice for close-up images.

- Consider using a large aperture to create a shallow depth of field. This will help isolate your subject from the background.

- A tripod will aid focusing and framing, but if you have to shoot handheld, try resting your elbows on the ground for stability.

▼ *Light is a key ingredient in flower photography—backlighting suits flowers and foliage, but bright, overcast light is often best for capturing blooms.*

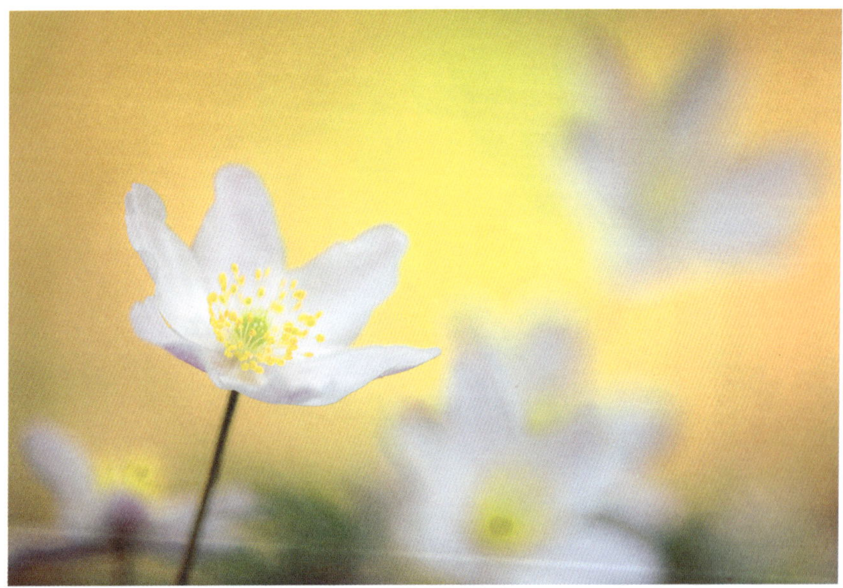

PETAL POWER

The abundance and diversity of flowers mean you don't need to venture far to create great images. You can find subjects in local woods, meadows, or your own garden. You can capture eye-catching floral images with basic kit, and they are ideal subjects for developing your close-up skills. For this assignment, head off to photograph a series of six images of flowers using different creative approaches.

Late spring and summer are best for flower photography in most places, but timing is important as you will want to photograph them when they are in peak condition. The window of opportunity is short—maybe just a day or two—so visit sites regularly to monitor the plants' progress and condition, and plan your visit for just the right time.

Most flowers are affected by wind movement, and, if they are being blown about, focusing and framing will be tricky. You could erect a windbreak made from a heavy-duty, clear polythene sheet, held in position by rods, for instance. However, it is often more practical to find subjects in sheltered positions, or simply to wait for a day with a predicted wind speed below 10mph (16kph).

Before setting up, study your subject from all angles, including a low, worm's-eye view (see page 26). Consider its surroundings and lighting and where exactly to position your camera. Even the smallest adjustments to your shooting angle can greatly alter the appearance of the flower and its background.

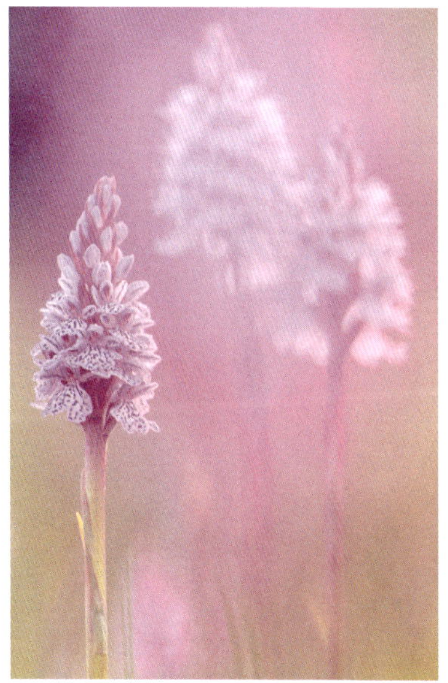

◀ Cloud cover acts like a giant soft-box, producing attractive, low-contrast light, and helping you to accurately record color and exquisite miniature details.

FIELD NOTES

• You may need to remove distracting grasses, twigs, and dead vegetation poking up in the background, using your fingers or scissors, before pressing the shutter. Be careful not to damage other flowers or rare plants, though.

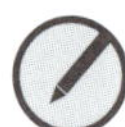
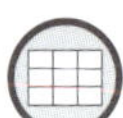
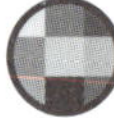

TECHNIQUE

- Mist will evaporate quickly as soon as the sun rises, so arrive on location early. You will need time to find your subject and position yourself for the most effective lighting and backgrounds.

- Watch the weather forecast carefully. You may need to make repeated visits before you find the optimum conditions. Pick a location that is easy to get to so that you can take advantage of any fleeting conditions that might occur.

- Don't be afraid of a wider view. Featuring your subject within a misty environment can be a great way of telling a story.

▼ *This mute swan was photographed from a distance so as to include the rays of light and the silhouettes of the branches. The backlighting has helped to emphasize the mist against the darker background.*

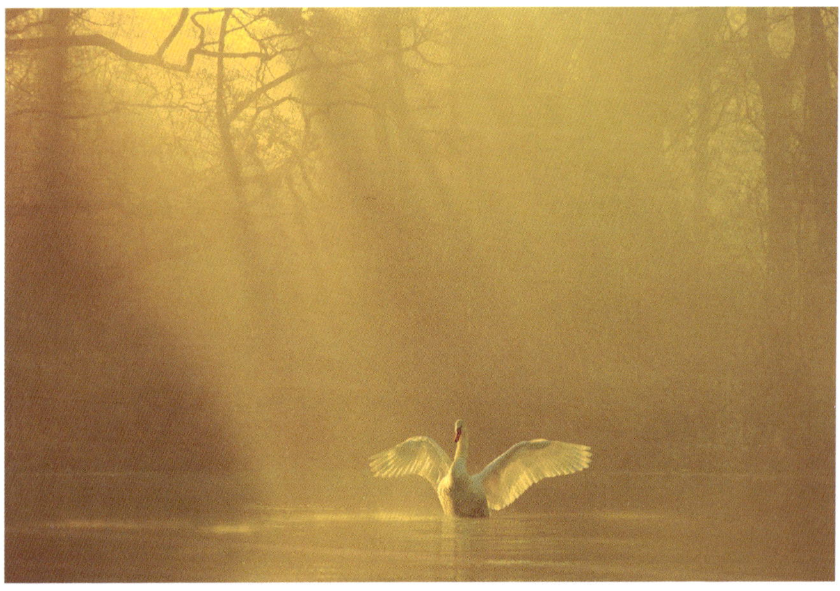

MIST OPPORTUNITY

Mist is most wildlife photographers' dream condition. It can be used to create an evocative atmosphere and add an air of mystery and intrigue to your images. Colors become muted and tones soften, allowing the form of the subject to take precedence.

In this assignment, we're asking you to capture a bird or animal in misty conditions. Focusing can become difficult when shooting in mist because of the reduced contrast levels. If you find your lens hunting and struggling to lock on to your subject, switch to manual focus. Of course, focusing will be much easier when your subject fills the frame, so also try shooting some close-up images. You will need to study the weather forecast and plan your shoots carefully to make the most of any fleeting opportunities.

See pages 102–3 for a guide to capturing great shots of birds in misty conditions. When you have completed your assignment, assemble your best shots and share them on your website or social media page (see page 122).

▼ *This lynx was photographed early one morning as mist hung in the woodland. The mist has reduced contrast and eliminated distractions from the background, helping to draw attention straight to the subject.*

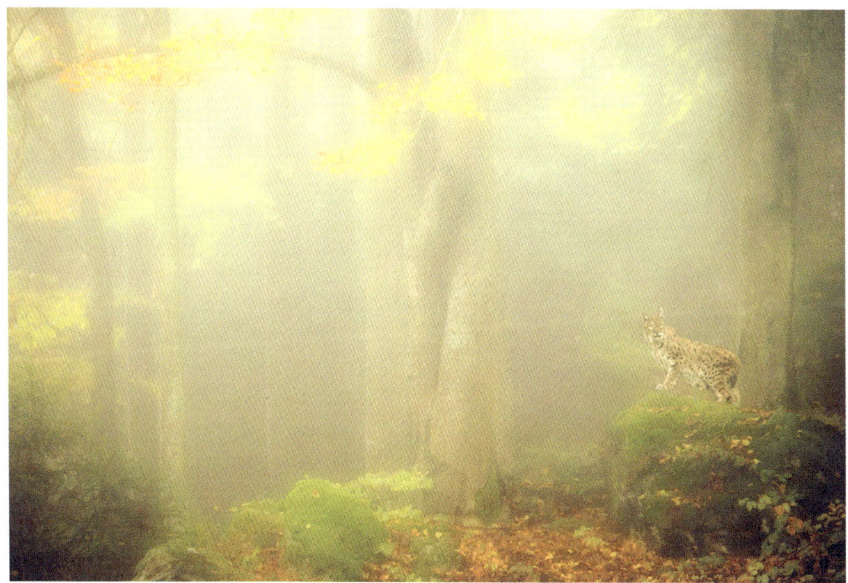

CAPTURE A BIRD

Birds on water provide the perfect subject for this assignment. Following a cold but clear night, mist will often form on ponds, lakes, and reservoirs the next morning.

• You will need to venture out early, as mist evaporates quickly as soon as the air starts to warm up. Arrive before dawn and assess the situation: look for where the birds are located and check the direction of the light.

• Any subject can look effective in mist, but some are more suitable than others. Birds with a distinctive shape work particularly well because their outline is immediately recognizable.

• Depending on the light, you may need to apply exposure compensation. In overcast conditions, try exposing to the right (see page 28) for a high-key effect—particularly effective with pale birds, such as swans.

• Most modern cameras allow the user to expand the focusing area, but for the most accurate focusing, use single-point focus instead and always try to keep this on the eyes of your subject.

▲ *The mist helped to reduce contrast, making it possible to shoot into the light and accentuate the form of the egret as it came in to land.*

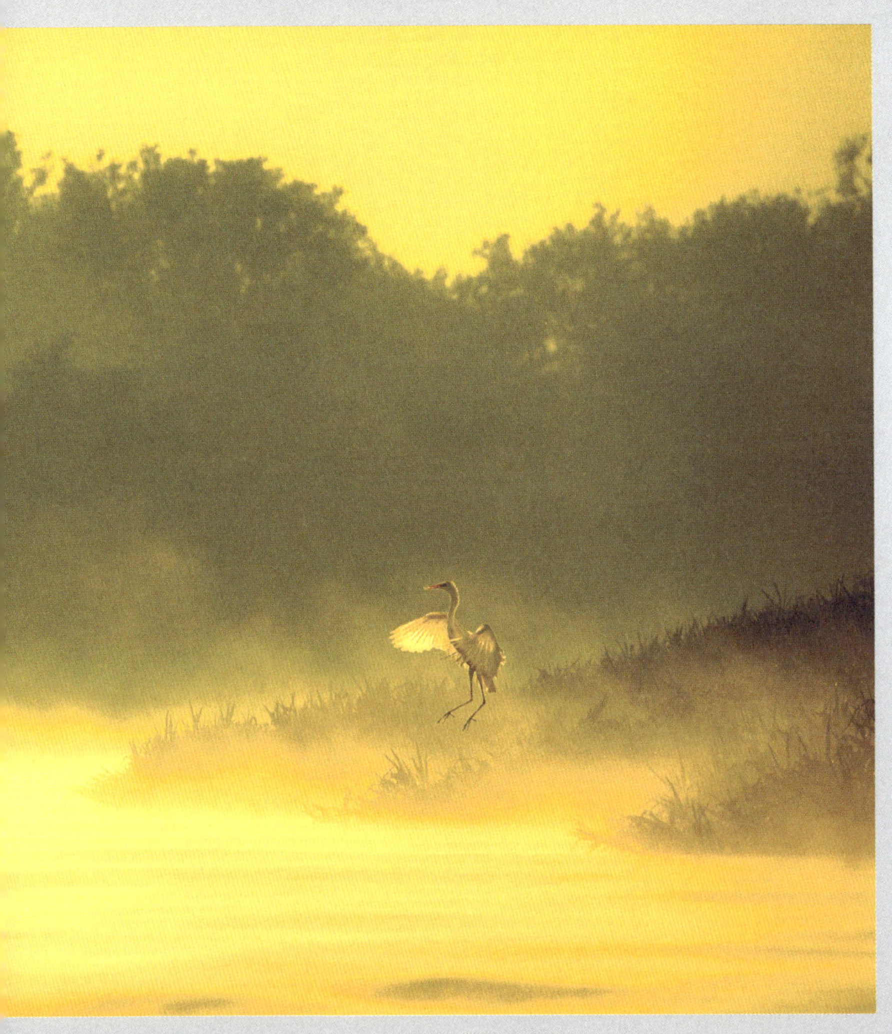

ASSIGNMENT JOURNAL

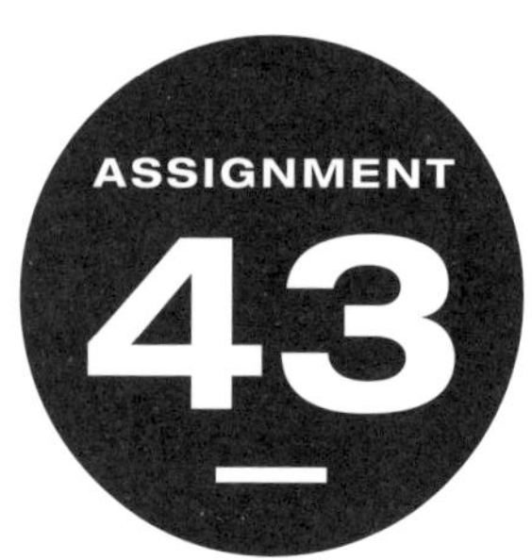

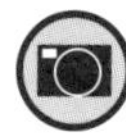

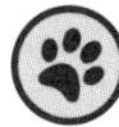

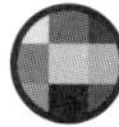

TECHNIQUE

- Make sure your ISO is set high enough to achieve a workable shutter speed. You will need to ensure your camera is fixed on a solid tripod.

- Use an external flash battery pack to allow you to fire a burst of images at a time, increasing your chances of success.

- A snoot is a tube that fits over a flashgun. This creates a spotlight effect, concentrating the light into a smaller area. It can be a useful addition to your kit bag and can be used to direct your flash more precisely.

CREATURES OF THE NIGHT

Photographing wildlife at night may sound daunting to some, but it doesn't need to be too complicated or highly technical. For this assignment, we would like you to head out under the cover of darkness and capture a set of three images exploring the wonders of nocturnal wildlife.

If you are attempting nighttime photography for the first time, keep it simple. Photography in darkness requires some sort of artificial light, which can be a continuous light source or flash. You will also need to keep your aperture wide open to let as much light into the camera as possible. Don't be afraid to raise your ISO—a relatively high setting will be needed to increase the sensitivity of the sensor. Even so, shutter speeds are likely to be much slower compared to shooting in natural light, so a tripod is also essential.

With a basic flash setup, you can use a feeding station (see page 14) and blind or hide (see page 56) to capture wildlife visiting your own garden.

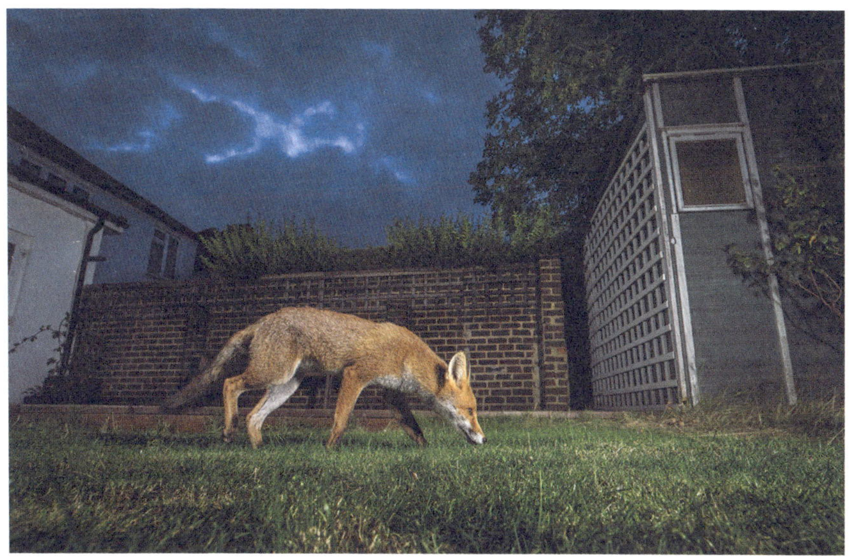

▲ *Even a back garden can provide plenty of opportunities for nighttime photography. Put out some bait regularly and you should be able to attract nocturnal wildlife, such as foxes.*

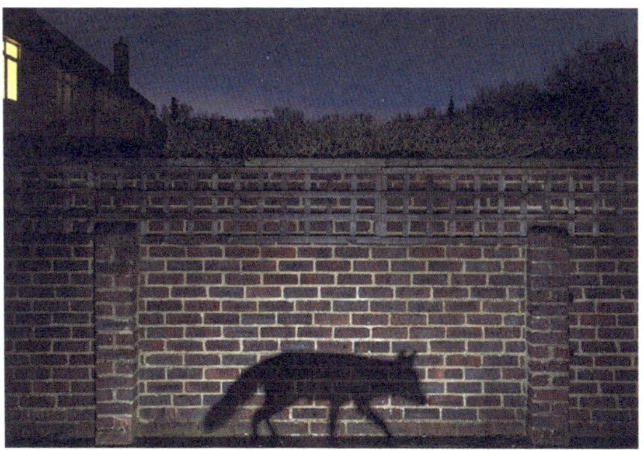

▲ *With careful positioning of your light source, you will find it possible to capture shadows.*

FIELD NOTES

- Don't be afraid to experiment with flash. The advantage of garden nighttime photography is that, over time, you can refine your setup to achieve more creative images.

- Don't ignore other possible light sources. Providing your ISO is set high enough, streetlamps, candles, or even moonlight can provide enough light for an image.

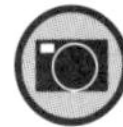
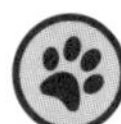
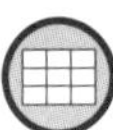
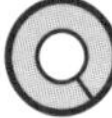

TECHNIQUE

- A macro is a good lens choice, but larger dragonflies can be photographed using a 300–400mm telephoto lens. With longer lenses, you can shoot from further away, minimizing the risk of disturbance.

- Increase ISO to generate a sufficiently fast shutter speed, particularly when working handheld or attempting to capture damselflies and dragonflies in flight.

DAMSELS IN DISTRESS

The spring and summer see the emergence of some of nature's most colorful, spectacular, and charismatic creatures—damselflies and dragonflies—and we want you to capture these beautiful insects. Dragonflies are timid and flighty and to get one within range of your close-up lens, you will need stealth and know-how. Visit marshes, swamps, lakes, ponds, and streams to find and observe them. They can be highly territorial, often patroling the same stretch of water and visiting the same perch again and again. Identify resting places, such as overhanging branches or reeds, and wait nearby, camera ready, for them to return.

Keep your camera parallel to your subject in order to place as much of it as possible within the lens's plane of focus. Dragonflies, with wings held open and perpendicular to their body, suit being photographed from directly overhead, to reveal the intricate veining of their wings. Most damselflies rest with their wings closed, so a side viewpoint generally works better. However, don't overlook less conventional or more creative angles. Head-on portraits emphasizing the insect's large eyes can look striking.

To complete this assignment, capture a series of eight images. Shoot portraits as well as behavior, such as hatching, mating, laying eggs, or flying. Finally, photograph something less conventional and more creative—close-ups of wing patterns (see page 54), or a damselfly in silhouette, perhaps. You'll learn much by varying your approach and technique in this way.

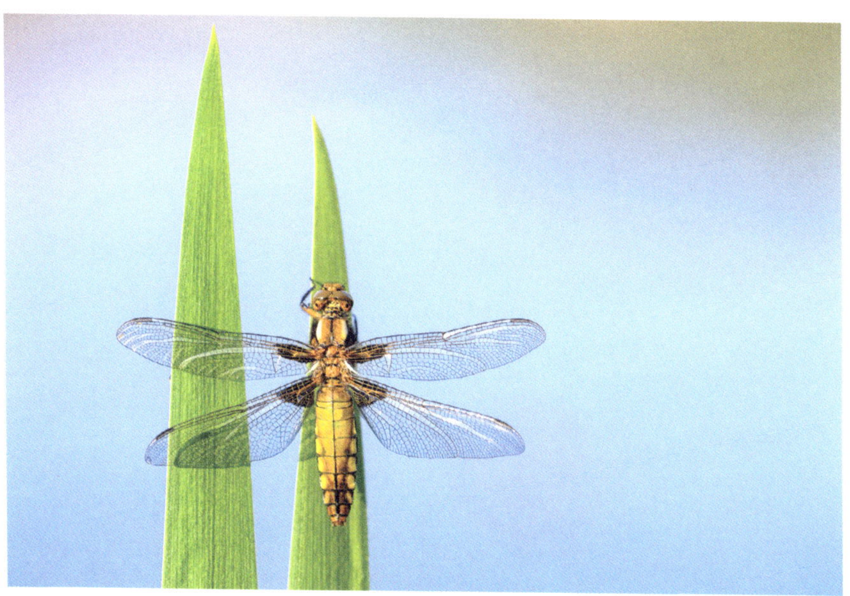

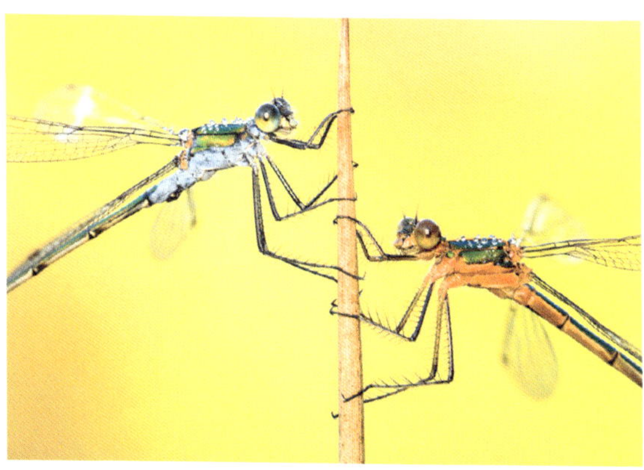

▲ The best times of day to photograph dragonflies and damselflies are morning and evening. When the temperatures are below 54°F (12°C), they will be less active and easier to approach.

◄ Look for roosting insects close to the water's edge, clinging to tall grasses or perched on branches.

FIELD NOTES

- Morning is a particularly good time for dragonfly photography, as tiny droplets of dew will form on the insect's wings and body during cool, clear nights. Droplets add interest, scale, and sparkle to your close-ups.

- Look for insects resting in a position where you can achieve a clean, uncluttered background.

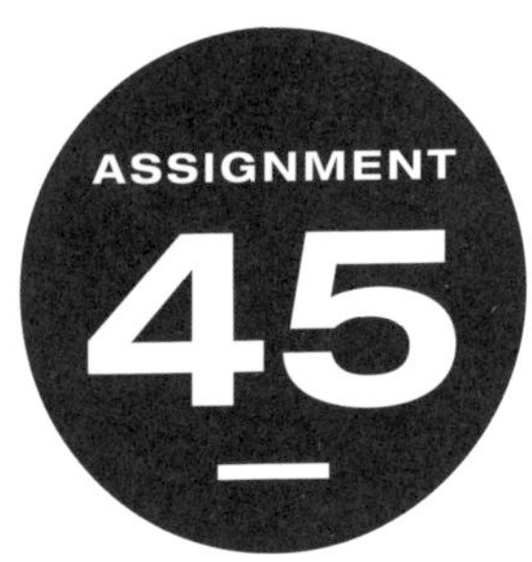

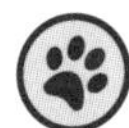
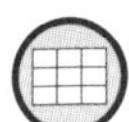

TECHNIQUE

- Calm, still days with a wind speed below 5mph (8kph) will typically prove best for photographing reflections, so check the forecast.

- It is often best to be close to the water's edge and shoot from a low perspective when photographing reflections, so consider your shooting angle carefully.

REFLECTING ON NATURE

Nature photographs that feature symmetrical, mirror-like reflections can be very striking, and evoke a feeling of tranquility. All you need to capture them is perfectly calm water and a willing subject.

Colorful reflections often provide the most interesting backgrounds. Sunny days with clear blue skies will produce vivid reflections, while warm, early-morning or late-evening light may render water golden and glowing. If you identify an area of reflective water that is particularly photogenic, sit and wait by the water's edge, camera at the ready, for a swan, heron, or duck to move into the right position.

Animals visiting waterholes to drink or bathe can also make good subjects. You could even create your own "reflection pool" in your garden for birds and animals to drink from—it only needs to be shallow, but the longer the better. Sink a pool into the ground, lined with heavy-duty black polythene, and build a small incline at the far end to encourage visiting birds to drink and bathe. Ensure you have a clean background and use a blind or hide (see page 56) or camouflage netting to disguise yourself. Dropping seed and mealworms at the water's edge will encourage birds to visit. Use a telephoto lens of about 300mm to capture your subject and its reflection.

To complete this project, capture five images, each of a different subject being reflected, and share them on your social media pages (see page 122).

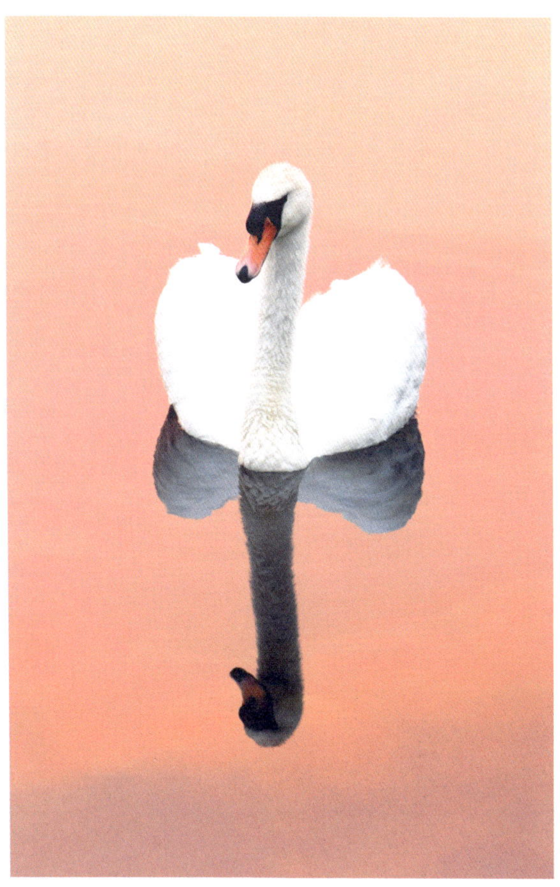

PRO TIPS

• Photographers are often told to avoid placing the horizon or subject centrally, but this can actually prove very effective when shooting a reflection. By keeping the space above and below your subject equidistant, you will capture images with eye-catching symmetry.

◀ *Warm, colorful skies at sunrise and sunset will provide beautiful, vivid reflections that will contrast with your subject.*

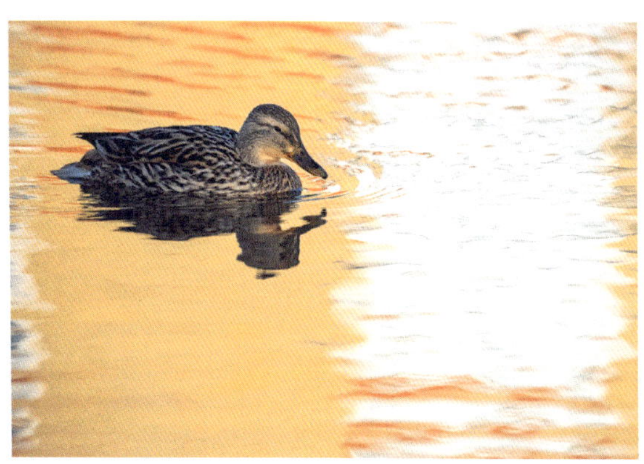

▲ *Nearby buildings can create abstract and colorful reflections in waterways. Urban wildlife tends to be accustomed to human activity and it is easier to get within picture-taking range.*

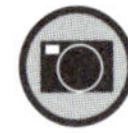
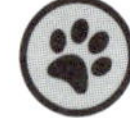
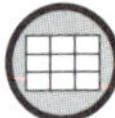

TECHNIQUE

- When capturing the behavior of a pair of animals, it is likely that your subjects will be moving. Use the predictive focus mode on your camera so you can track their movements.

- Keep your camera set to high-speed drive mode and fire bursts of images to help you capture the perfect moment.

- Use a notebook to jot down times, locations and behavior. You will soon begin to notice patterns. This knowledge will help when it comes to planning your shoots.

▼ *Images that depict behavior give a real insight into the life of the subject.*

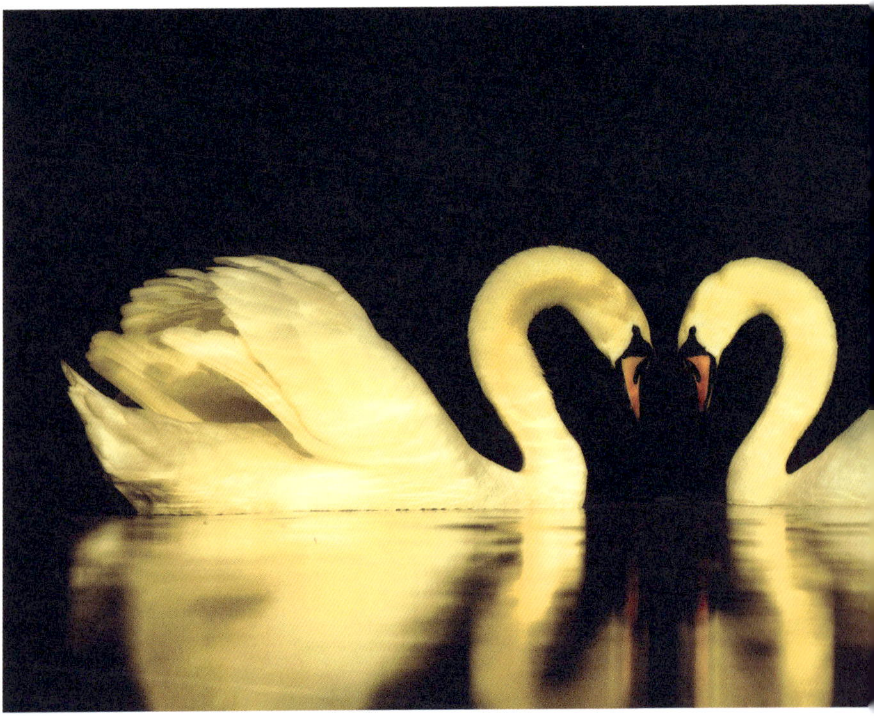

TWO BY TWO

Images that depict wildlife behavior, such as a breeding pair of birds or animals in courtship display, bonding, or passing food to each other—at a crucial time in their life cycle—tell a story and offer a glimpse into their world. Your assignment is to seek out a suitable pair of birds or animals and spend time observing them, with the ultimate aim of capturing a series of six images that depict their breeding behavior. This will no doubt take both time and effort, but the rewards will certainly be worth it.

As wildlife photographers, it is our duty and responsibility to protect and preserve the subjects that we photograph, and ensure we do not disturb them or cause them distress in any way. In addition, in many countries you will need to obtain a licence to photograph certain listed bird species on or near their nests, for instance. It is essential that you check with local regulatory bodies and conservation groups for details of the laws governing nature photography in your country, and make sure you are familiar and comply with them at all times. The guidance for this assignment continues on pages 112–13.

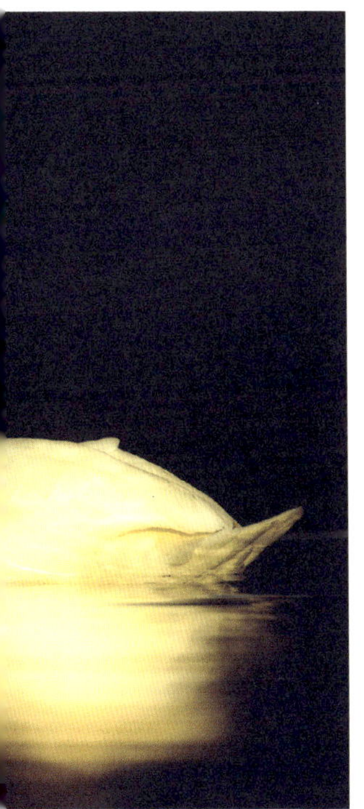

ASSIGNMENT JOURNAL

SHOOTING A PAIR

Waterbirds, such as swans, grebes, or ducks, make ideal subjects for photographing in pairs. Often stunning birds, they are numerous and sometimes provide elaborate courtship displays that offer opportunities for exciting compositions.

• Try to avoid being too ambitious when deciding on your subjects. Stick to a species that is easy to find, local, and always present.

• Spend time observing behavioral patterns. This is an important part of wildlife photography and it will help you to be in the right place at the right time.

• When shooting birds on water, a wide aperture will result in a shallow depth of field, helping to blur the foreground and background, separating the subject from any potential distractions behind.

• Think about whether it would help to build a floating blind or hide to help you get closer (see page 59).

• Concentrate on just one pair of birds and follow them for as long as possible.

• In order to freeze animals or birds in motion, you must be prepared. It is important to have your camera at the ready at all times, and set a fast enough shutter speed to freeze the action—at least 1/800 sec.

• Consider your shooting angle. An angle low to the water will give you an intimate view of waterbirds, as well as helping to blur the foreground and background. A beanbag is often the most effective support, offering both stability and excellent freedom of movement.

▲ *Shooting at water level has resulted in a view of the subjects at their eye level, bringing the viewer into their world, as well as creating a diffused and distraction-free foreground and background to focus attention on the subjects.*

▶ *Freezing action demands a fast shutter speed—this image was shot at 1/2000 sec. to ensure both birds were rendered pin-sharp.*

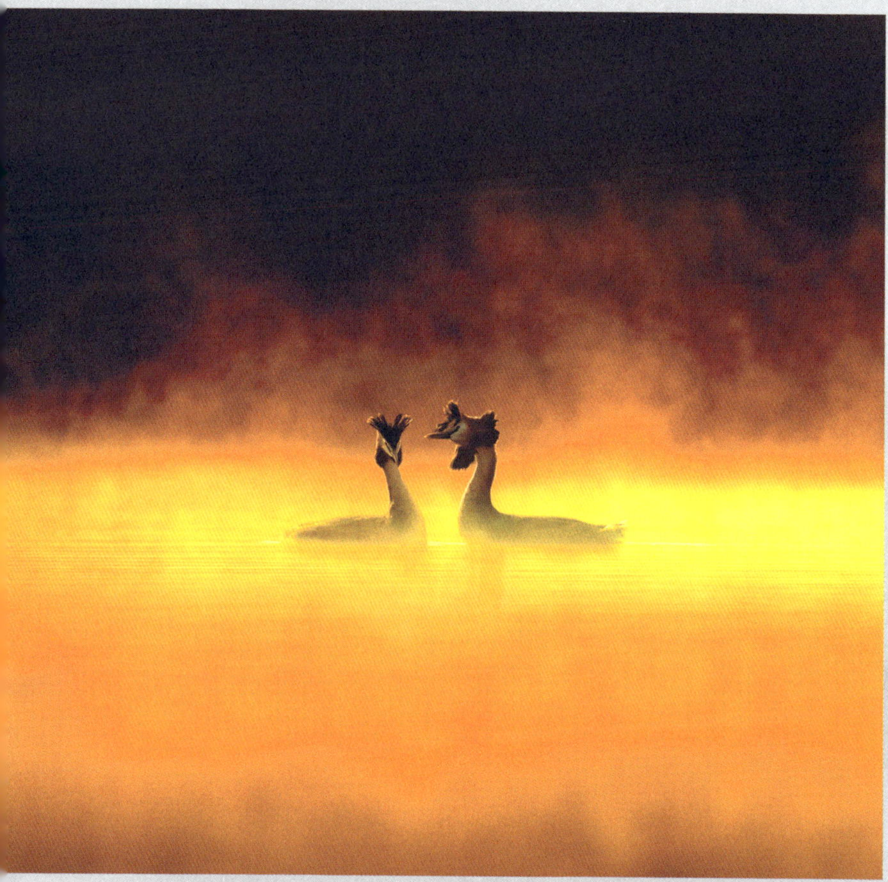

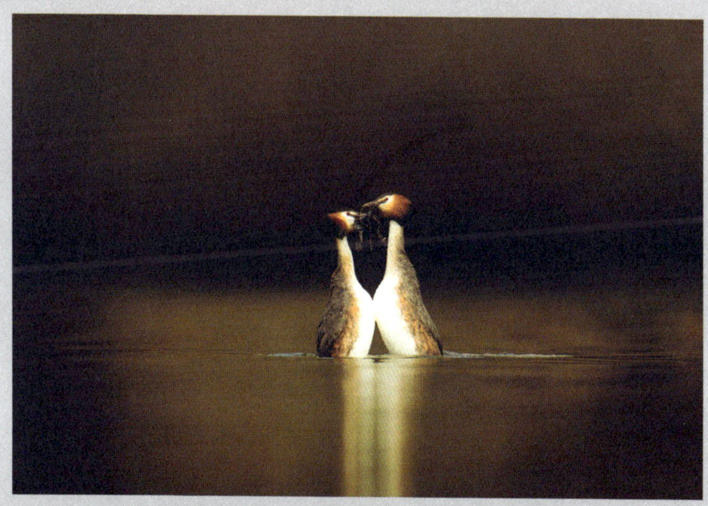

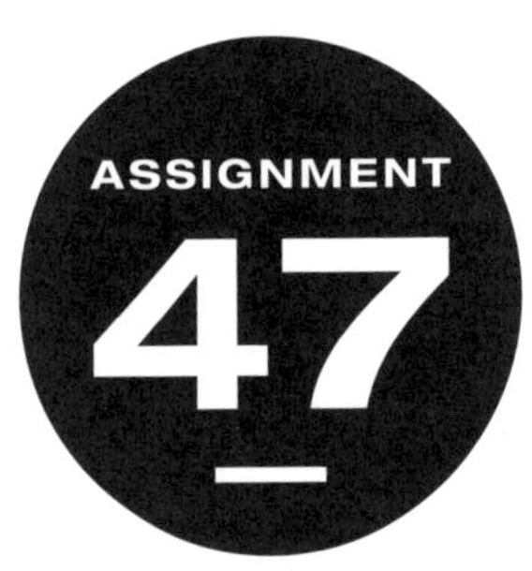

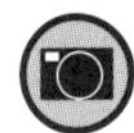

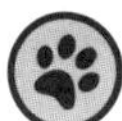
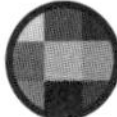

TECHNIQUE

- Ensure you have adequate buoyancy and diving skills before trying this assignment.

- You can take images while snorkeling or even in rock pools at low tide.

- Shoot from your subject's eye level to keep images looking natural. A low perspective, looking up from slightly beneath a subject helps isolate it from its background.

- Minimize the amount of water between you and your subject—get as close as possible, ideally within 3ft (1m). This will give you better color, contrast, and sharpness.

- Don't get obsessed with the technical stuff. Keep things basic and just enjoy getting a feel for underwater photography.

UNDERWATER WORLD

Once upon a time, underwater photography was limited to those with specialized and expensive kit. However, underwater compacts and sports cameras such as GoPro, along with polycarbonate housings for conventional cameras, have made it possible for everyone to capture stunning images of the extraordinary wildlife under the waves. For this assignment, buy or borrow an inexpensive underwater compact camera, new or used, and find somewhere safe to explore under the water.

Underwater photography provides a number of fresh challenges not found on land. Most significantly, water absorbs more light and color the deeper you go, with reds being filtered out faster than blues. To capture your subject's true color, you will need a strobe (a type of flash) or your shots will appear very blue. Most compact underwater cameras have built-in flash. However, beware of backscatter caused by light illuminating tiny particles in the water—using an external strobe positioned to one side of the lens is the best way to avoid this. Good results are still possible without artificial light, but you need to remain close to the surface to ensure there is sufficient light, ideally coming from over your shoulder. Create four images to begin with. You never know, this could be the start of a new passion.

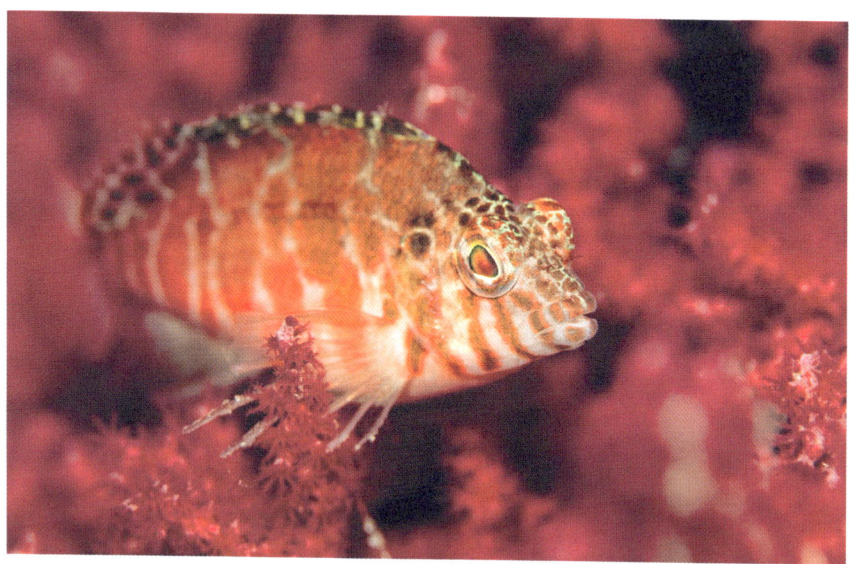

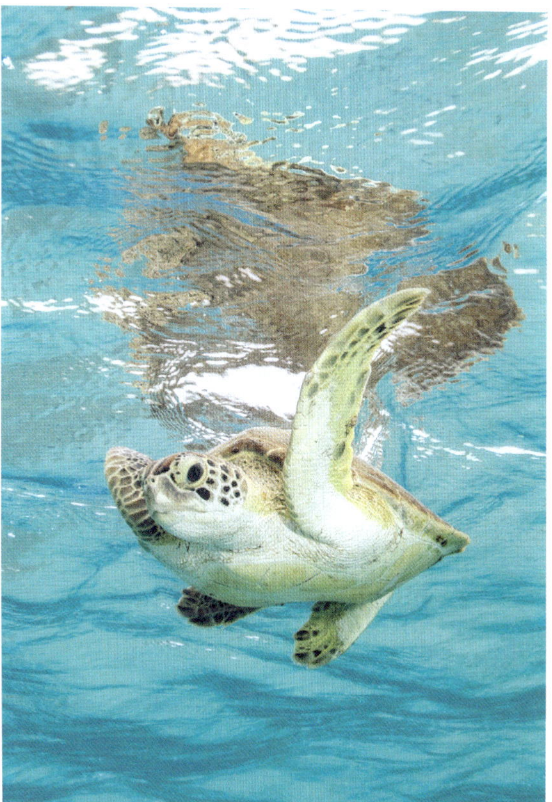

▲ Close-ups are a good way to begin underwater photography. You can reveal colorful and secretive little aquatic creatures that are normally ignored.

◀ Spending time with a single subject will help you capture better images. A wideangle lens is ideal for photographing larger fish or marine animals, such as this turtle, but you may need a specialist underwater lens.

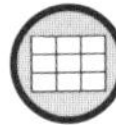

TECHNIQUE

- Use shutter priority and experiment with different shutter speeds to find the most pleasing result. Start with 1 sec. or even slower, and increase this to see the effects it has on the images.

- Use your camera's high-speed drive mode and fire several bursts of images. The beauty of intentional camera movement (ICM) is that no two images are exactly alike. Having several to choose from will increase your chances of success.

- One benefit of working with slow shutter speeds is that they allow you to use a low ISO. Take advantage of this to extract the best possible quality from your images.

LEARN TO PAINT

There are several ways to use movement creatively in nature photography. Intentional camera movement (ICM) is a technique frequently used in landscape photography to create abstract or impressionistic interpretations of a scene, and we can also apply it to wildlife photography. We'd like you to experiment with intentionally moving the camera during an exposure and seeing what effects this has on your images. Use the camera like a paintbrush and experiment with different types of movement and a variety of shutter speeds.

Color can play a big part in the success of an ICM image, so pay careful attention to your surroundings and look for colorful backgrounds to shoot toward. Try to contrast the subject with the background as this will make the motion more obvious in the image. Remember that the subject doesn't have to be moving; static birds and animals work well, too.

The key here is to experiment as much as possible and create combinations that you find the most esthetically pleasing. There are no rights or wrongs when it comes to this type of photography. To complete the assignment, create three completely different images of different subjects, and see how innovative you can be.

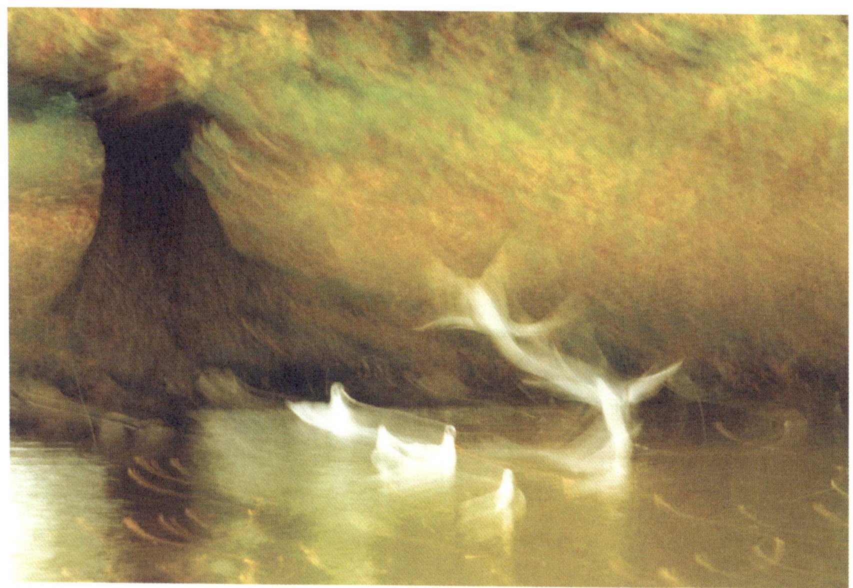

▲ This image shows a black-headed gull taking off against a fall backdrop. A shutter speed of 0.5 sec. coupled with the deliberate movement of the camera can create the appearance of an Impressionist painting.

▼ Your subject doesn't always need to be recognizable for the image to work. A shutter speed of 0.4 sec. and some intentional camera movement has recorded the motion of these gulls as they took off from the water.

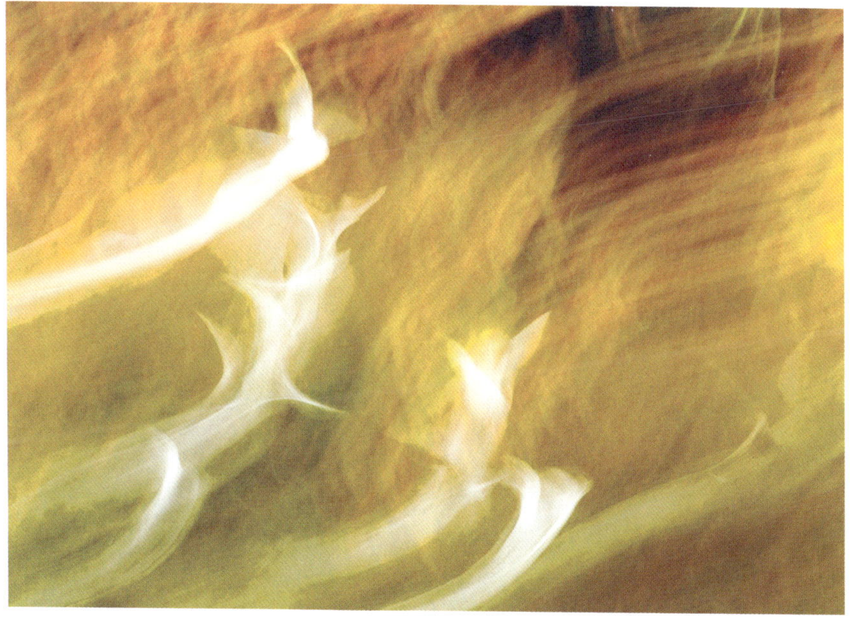

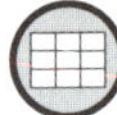

TECHNIQUE

- Observe your subjects carefully to pick up patterns in behavior, which will help you park your vehicle in the ideal spot.

- Find quiet areas on the road where you can park safely and wait—patience is the name of the game. The more time you spend in one particular spot, the more chance you have of capturing a memorable shot.

- For ground-level subjects, try crouching by the side of your vehicle and covering yourself in scrim netting to disguise your shape.

PRO TIP

- Choosing the right kind of camera support is essential when shooting from a vehicle. We recommend using a beanbag as it can be placed over a car's windowsill and will provide a solid support for even the biggest lenses.

▼ *This image was taken from a parked car at the side of the road. The grouse was uphill, so an eye-level angle was achieved relatively easily, adding intimacy.*

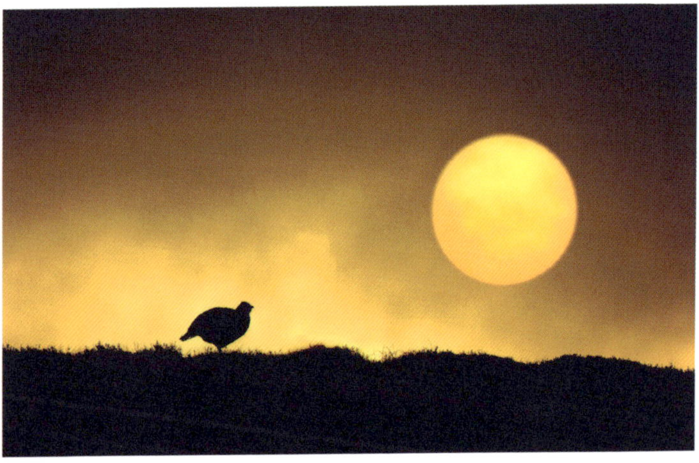

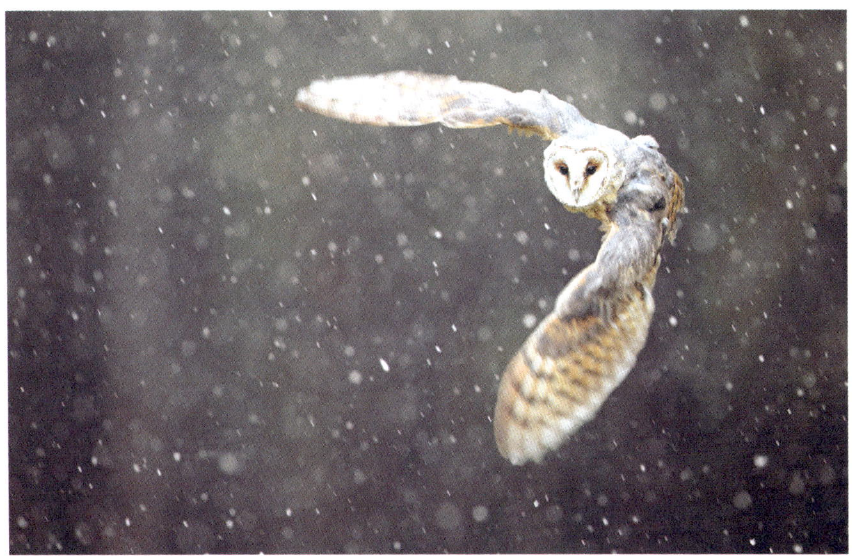

▲ *This flight shot of a barn owl was captured by pulling the car up close to the bird's hunting ground.*

ROADRUNNER

One of the most difficult aspects of wildlife photography is getting close enough to your subject to capture good portraits. With species that are very wary of humans, you will need to use a blind or hide (see page 56) to be able to enter their "fear circle"—the invisible perimeter that you can approach without them taking fright. While most wild animals regard the human shape as a threat, they do not see vehicles in the same way; a car can often enter a subject's fear circle without any reaction from it. So, for this project, you will be shooting from the comfort of your vehicle and using it as a mobile blind.

First, become familiar with your location. Look for roads that are quiet and frequented by birds and mammals, and visit regularly to work out when to visit with your camera. Dawn is usually the most productive time as wildlife tends to be more active during the early hours of the day, and there will also be less traffic on the roads. There is an abundance of wildlife that can be found at the roadside, from hunting birds of prey to grouse, waders, rabbits, and hares. Park safely and wait. Be patient enough and you should find your subjects fairly easy to photograph.

Shoot a set of four images of different birds or animals from your vehicle. You will find this is a very effective approach for photographing wildlife, and you will probably return to it often.

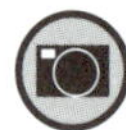
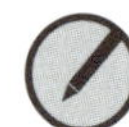
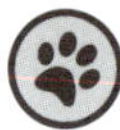
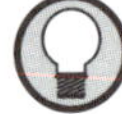

TECHNIQUE

- When traveling by plane, pack your camera equipment in your hand luggage. This is sometimes easier said than done as weight is always an issue. Never put a camera or lens in a bag in the airplane's hold as there is a high risk of it being damaged.

- Working abroad means it's difficult to pop back if you are not happy with results. So, before attempting creative techniques, first capture some "insurance shots."

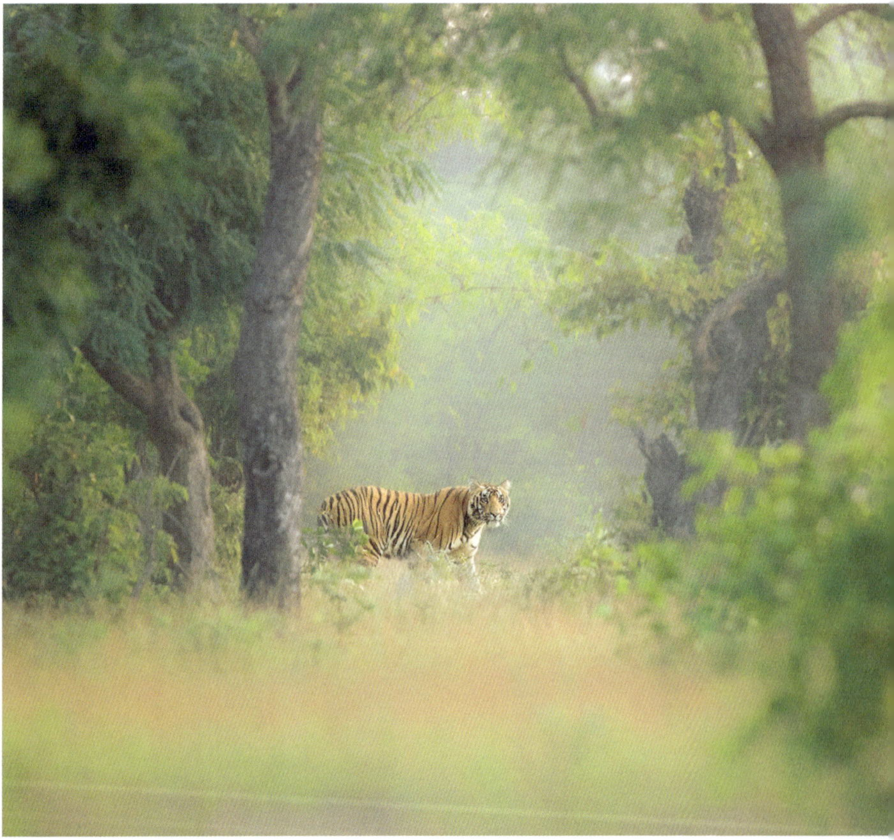

BIG GAME

Planning an overseas nature photography trip can seem daunting. It is likely to be an expensive endeavor, but it will be well worth the time, effort, and cost. Carry out plenty of research before you go, to become familiar with your potential subjects and environment. Study online pictures of the region to get an idea of what is possible, but try to think about new ways to portray the local species. If possible, speak to other photographers who have visited the location, to gain insider knowledge.

When planning your trip, we recommend staying in just one or two locations, rather than trying to fit in too much. It is also a good idea before you travel to book a local guide who knows the area and the wildlife. It will be money well spent. A good guide should be able to get you into the right positions at the right times, and be competent at identifying and tracking the animals. When you arrive, it will take time to adjust to your new environment, so try not to put too much pressure on yourself. Once you have spent a couple of days settling in and getting to know your subjects, you will be in a much better position to capture successful images.

To complete this assignment, assemble a portfolio of the very best images from your holiday. You may even decide to make a photobook of them.

◄ *This tiger was photographed in India with a 300mm f/2.8 lens. This focal length was ideal for capturing the animal in its environment. The image would not have worked so well with a longer lens.*

PRO TIPS

- Research your destination and the behavior of possible subjects before you travel.

- It is often difficult to know what opportunities might arise on a trip somewhere new, so take several lenses of different focal lengths and be prepared for every eventuality. Long lenses are useful for isolating your subject, but wideangle lenses can be used to show your subject in its habitat.

- One handy tip for traveling light is to take an empty beanbag, and buy some rice or lentils to fill it up when you arrive at your destination.

TECHNIQUE

- To create your own website, you need to purchase a domain name, typically consisting of your name, followed by "photography", for example, joebloggsphotography.com. Try 123Reg, GoDaddy, or Namecheap—you can normally buy a domain for a modest annual fee.

- Only share your very best images—you have just one chance to make a good first impression.

- Add a Contact page to your website to help you connect with visitors and also encourage sales enquiries.

SHOWTIME

Having captured so many great nature images by completing the assignments in this book, you need somewhere to showcase them. You might decide to print and frame them for your own enjoyment, or enter them into competitions (see page 124). However, the most popular method of showing images today is to build a website, or your own social media page. For this project, we want you to create a platform for your nature photography portfolio.

A website is the most obvious way to create an online presence, but you don't need to understand code to create a professional-looking site. A web builder—such as Photium, Squarespace, or Wix—offers hundreds of easily customizable templates that make creating a unique-looking site easy and affordable. Some also allow you to sell prints through your website.

If populating an entire website feels too daunting, you can set up your own social media page instead. Instagram is a great platform for photography, but don't overlook 500px, Facebook, or Flickr. You can also display images in high resolution on Vero Social. Social media pages encourage interaction with other photographers and may lead to picture sales and even commercial opportunities. Once you have established your online presence, the project is complete.

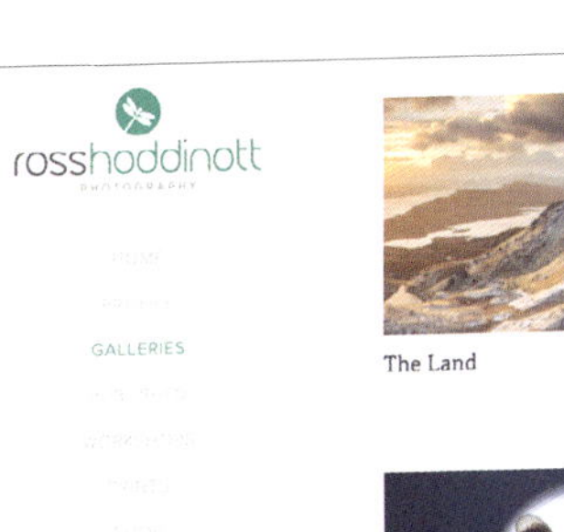
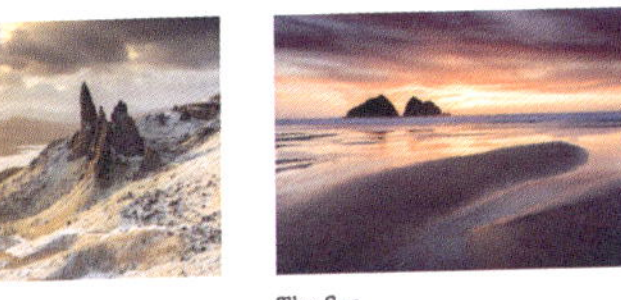
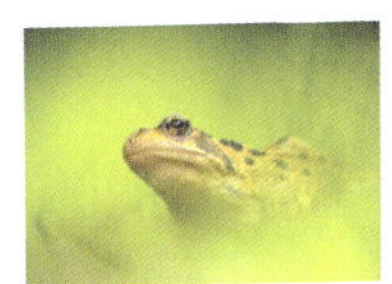

The Land

The Sea

British Wildlife

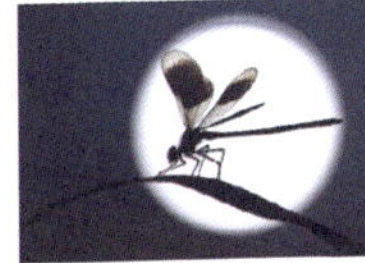
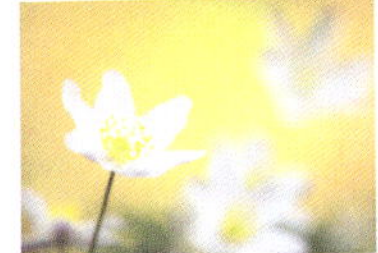
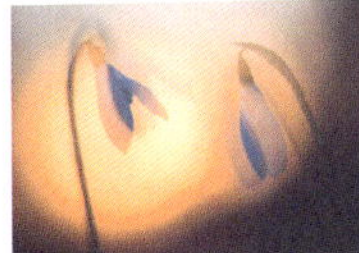
Six legs

Plantlife

Creative Visions

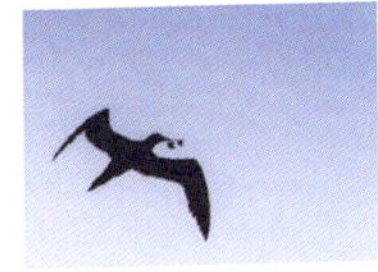
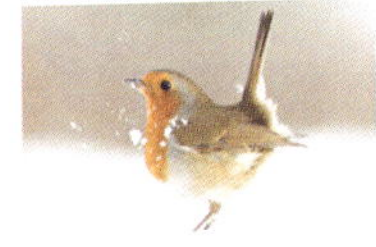
The Galapagos Islands

Awards

▲ Keep the layout of your website clean and simple, with minimal text—let your photographs do the talking.

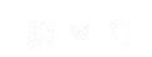
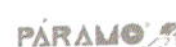
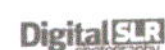
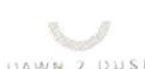
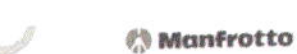

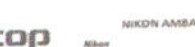
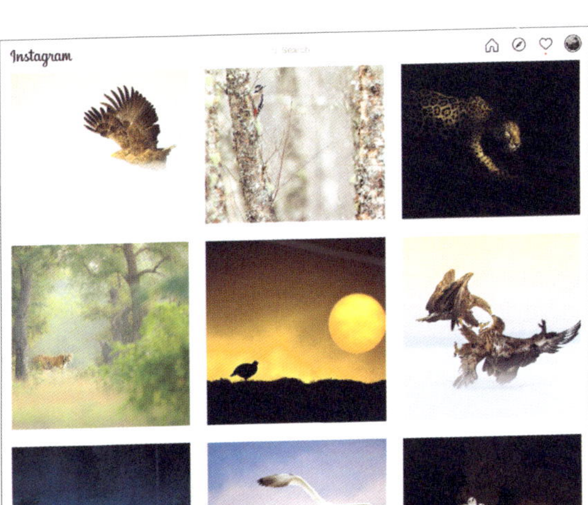

◄ Having a social media presence is one of the easiest and most effective ways to showcase your portfolio of images.

PRO TIP

- The more pages you build, over multiple platforms, the greater the exposure you'll create for your images. Update your content regularly.

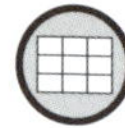

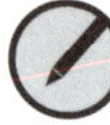

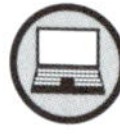

TECHNIQUE

- Photography competition judges are looking for images that offer something a bit different, not imitations of previously successful compositions.

- Enter images that have immediate impact, are unusual, creative, or innovative in some way, or highlight unusual wildlife behavior. These will always stand out to judges and do best in competitions.

- Competitions run by photography communities typically provide feedback and guidance, and entering these will help you grow and develop your creativity.

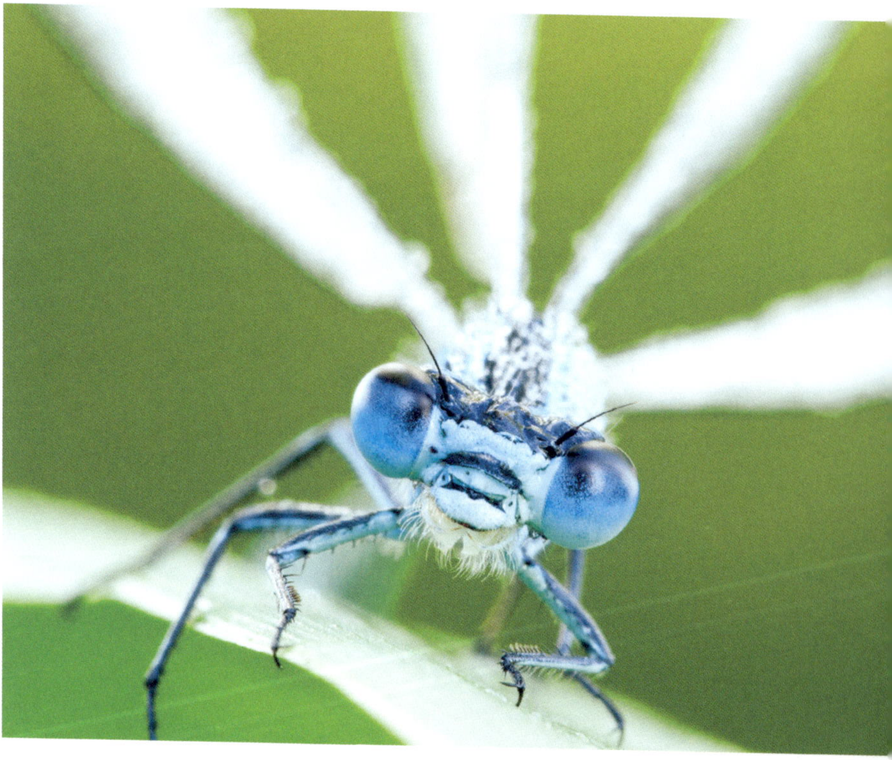

NATURAL SELECTION

There is no shortage of nature photography competitions where you can pit your work against that of other photographers from around the world. Competitions can be rewarding to enter and help your creative development. Wildlife Photographer of the Year is the best-known nature photography contest in the world, attracting over 50,000 entries annually, but there are many others. A number of photography magazines and some photography community websites run their own contests.

Before you enter your most prized images, however, you should consider the potential benefits and pitfalls. Prizes and exposure are the two big incentives if you are successful, while being commended also reassures you that your images have widespread appeal. However, competitions are very subjective and unpredictable. Regardless of how good your photographs are, there are never any guarantees, so if you do enter you must be equally prepared to be unsuccessful. Winning competitions should not be viewed as a way of measuring the quality of your work, just the cherry on top if you do succeed.

So, for this final assignment, we want you to research and enter a suitable nature photography competition. Perhaps start off by entering one that provides feedback on entries, as this will help you to learn what judges are looking for. Enjoy looking through your files and shortlisting your entry. View your work critically and objectively. Good luck!

ASSIGNMENT JOURNAL

◄ *Images with immediate impact have a far better chance of grabbing the judges' attention.*

First published 2020 by
Ammonite Press
an imprint of Guild of Master Craftsman Publications Ltd
Castle Place, 166 High Street, Lewes, East Sussex, BN7 1XU,
United Kingdom

Text and images © Ross Hoddinott and Ben Hall, 2020, with the exception of the
following images: p105 all images © Richard Peters www.richardpeters.co.uk,
p115 all images © Keith Lyall and Jo Horrocks www.kclyall.co.uk

Copyright in the Work © GMC Publications Ltd, 2020

Reprinted 2024

ISBN 978 1 78145 405 3

All rights reserved.

The rights of Ross Hoddinott and Ben Hall to be identified as the authors of this
work have been asserted in accordance with the Copyright, Designs, and Patents
Act 1988, Sections 77 and 78.

No part of this publication may be reproduced, stored in a retrieval system,
or transmitted in any form or by any means without the prior permission
of the publishers and copyright owners.

The publishers and authors can accept no legal responsibility for any
consequences arising from the application of information, advice, or instructions
given in this publication.

A catalog record for this book is available from the British Library.

Publisher: Jason Hook
Art Director: Robin Shields
Designer: Luke Herriott
Editor: Rob Yarham

Color reproduction by GMC Reprographics

Printed and bound in China

How was the book?
Please post your
feedback and photos:
#52AssignmentsNature

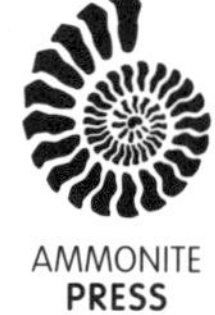

AMMONITE
PRESS

ammonitepress.com

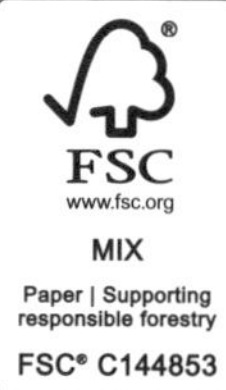